Introduction

This book is about a famous victory. It tells the tale of how a group of people took on the might of the aviation industry, international business and the UK Government and won. It is the story of how plans for the massive expansion of Heathrow Airport, including a third runway, were stopped. The book outlines the strategy and the tactics used. It is an inspiring story. It is a very human story. But it also contains valuable lessons for campaigners wherever they live and whatever their cause.

Inevitably it is written from my perspective. It is the campaign through my eyes; told in my words. The ideal would have been for all the people involved in the campaign to have contributed to the book. That would have reflected the diversity of the campaign. But that wouldn't have been practicable! In due course other books will be written about the campaign. Academics will analyse it. Historians will put it into perspective. More people will tell their stories. The local authorities and lawyers will have valuable insights to add. This book is essentially written from a campaigners' perspective while events were still fresh in people's minds. The opinions expressed, the words used, any errors that may have crept in, are all mine and should not be attributed to anybody else.

I hope you enjoy it!

John Stewart

	Contents
Page 4	Getting started
Page 5	Putting in place a national campaign
Page 12	The Heathrow Campaign
Page 14	The role of direct action
Page 16	The coalition takes shape
Page 26	Plane Stupid is born
Page 33	The official consultation starts
Page 36	Post-consultation: the need to maintain momentum
Page 41	January 2009: the Government gives green light to expansion
Page 42	Our response
Page 46	AirportWatch in 2009
Page 48	2010 brings a surprise and then victory
Page 50	Reflections on the campaign

A third runway at Heathrow was what the aviation industry in the UK wanted above all else. This book tells the story of how they were stopped.

Getting Started

When we set out on our historic campaign to stop Heathrow expansion nearly a decade ago a victory party would have seemed like a dream. But our triumph was no fluke. It wasn't a question of luck. It was the result of a clear strategy, a radical approach, daring tactics and an utter refusal to believe that we wouldn't win.

1997: Early Beginnings

Although the actual campaign against the third runway didn't begin until 2002, we were aware in 1997 a new runway might be on the cards. There were clear signs Tony Blair's newly-elected Labour Government would go for a national programme of airport expansion. In 1997 the economy was strong and the demand for budget flights, in particular, was growing. Moreover, the new Government was showing little sympathy towards people living around airports and under flight paths. Its first Aviation Minister, the former Oscar-winning actress turned politician, Glenda Jackson, was regarded as a close friend of the aviation industry.

There were signs, too, that the industry had considerable influence over the new Government. To celebrate the Millennium on midnight January 1st 2000, Tony Blair joined Bob Ayling, the boss of British Airways, on top of London's latest tourist attraction, the London Eye, paid for by......British Airways. But celebration that night was the last thing on the minds of the countless people living under Heathrow's flight paths, with jets roaring over their homes, sometimes at a rate of one every ninety seconds. All I could think about as I lay under the bedclothes, the fan heater whirring in an attempt to mask the noise of the incessant aircraft, was the missed opportunity. What if we had climbed the London Eye that evening and unfurled banners from the top? But our campaign wasn't yet ready for it. Direct action was still a few years away.

We had friends in government. For six years, until he was sacked, Michael Meacher, the Secretary of State for the Environment, fought a valiant battle to get the Government to take sustainability and noise issues seriously. The left-winger, Chris Mullin, who succeeded Glenda Jackson as Aviation Minister did his best. Shortly after leaving the job he penned these memorable words: "I learnt two things. First, that the demands of the aviation industry are insatiable. Second, that successive governments have usually given way to them." He added, "Although nowadays the industry pays lip-serve to the notion of sustainability, its demands are essentially unchanged. It wants more of everything - airports, runways, terminals."

We knew we had to start planning early to have any chance of defeating plans for the expansion

Within the Labour Party there were many individuals, including MPs and Peers, who shared Mullin's view. The Government as a whole, though, was set on expansion. We knew we had to start planning our strategy straightaway if we were to have a chance of defeating any plans for the expansion of Heathrow and the other airports the Government might draw up. In my experience pressure groups often fail simply because they start campaigning too late in the day. Sometimes that is inevitable as local people may only hear of plans at the last minute. But success is much more likely if campaigners can map out a long-term strategy. When planning for big projects like new runways or new roads business and the civil service think many years ahead. We need to try to match that.

1997: Our First Meetings

In 1997, the campaigners from Heathrow, Stansted and Gatwick started meeting with a handful of national environmental organisations to discuss joint working. During the 1990s many of these national groups had established a good record of joint working on transport issues. Usually they had been brought together by Transport 2000, the country's premier transport lobbying organisation, and its Director of more than twenty years, Stephen Joseph. It was Transport 2000 which first suggested that the three airport campaign groups start discussing aviation with some of the national environmental organisations working in the field.

"The demands of the aviation industry are insatiable.....successive governments have usually given way to them." **Chris Mullin, former Aviation Minister**

Putting in Place a National Campaign

2000: AirportWatch, a national umbrella body, is formed

In 2000 these early discussions resulted in the formation of AirportWatch. It was a national umbrella body which aimed to bring together the campaign groups around the different airports and the national environmental organisations opposed to airport expansion. It called for a demand management approach to aviation rather than one of aggressive expansion.

> **AirportWatch had five key jobs to do.**
>
> 1. **Unite all the campaign groups**
>
> 2. **Ensure the issue of aviation expansion became a national debate and went top of the political agenda**
>
> 3. **Influence the outcome of that debate, particularly around:**
>   - **Economics**
>   - **Climate Change**
>   - **Climate Justice**
>   - **Noise**
>   - **Community Destruction**
>
> 4. **Build links with campaigners in Europe**
>
> 5. **Counter the influence of civil servants**

1. Unite all the campaign groups

Our first task was to ensure that the campaign groups from all the airports were united. We had to make it clear that none of us was in the business of suggesting that expansion should take place at somebody else's airport. That had happened in the past. It led to failure. Quite rightly, campaigners had been called NIMBYS (Not in My Backyard). If we simply opposed expansion at our own airports, we would be fighting forever with one arm behind our backs. Only if we stood together would we be in a position to make what we believed were the strong economic, social and environmental arguments against airport expansion.

I feel this has been fundamental to our success but I am aware it is a position which engenders a lot of debate. Clearly if there are circumstances where there is a need for more capacity, choices have to be made about where the expansion takes place. There may be an argument for some growth in some 'developing' countries, (although much of the drive for expansion in those countries may simply be a desire to match the pretty disastrous flying habits of the more developed world). In somewhere like Europe or America, the case for extra capacity is very doubtful. Much of the demand has been created by the tax-breaks and other subsidies aviation receives, leading to artificially low fares. 45% of air trips within Europe are 500 kilometres or less in length. Many of those trips would transfer to a fast, affordable rail service if it were in place, or, in the case of business, could be replaced by the ever more sophisticated technology available for video-conferencing. A lot of capacity would be freed up. Growth in demand for aviation is not inevitable. In fact,

All groups opposed expansion plans at all airports. This position creates a lot of debate but was a key factor in our success

in the long-term, it is unlikely. Concerns about climate change and rising oil prices are likely to limit aviation growth. Emissions from aviation are already threatening to destroy government targets to tackle climate change. And oil prices, despite a recent dip during the recession, will continue to climb as the fields from which oil can be extracted relatively cheaply begin to dry up.

In my view this all means that the aviation industry in the rich world should be planning for decline rather than pursuing unrealistic dreams of expansion. Governments, instead of giving aviation tax-breaks like tax-free fuel, should be providing fiscal incentives which encourage people to travel by rail and businesses to use video-conferencing. A forward-looking fiscal policy would also facilitate the development of green industries which could be the mainstay of our future economy and provide employment for many of the workers displaced from declining industries such as aviation.

AirportWatch also had to wrestle with a slightly different capacity question. What if a new airport was simply *replacing* an existing one, rather than creating additional capacity? For many years in the UK the idea of building an off-shore airport to replace Heathrow, and maybe also Stansted and Gatwick, has been talked about. The most likely site would be off the Kent and Essex coasts in South-East England. The idea has its supporters. A number of people living under the flight paths to Heathrow, for example, are in favour of it. Understandably so. It would remove or reduce the torrent of noise over their heads. But the airport would also bring problems. It would

We took the view that only by opposing expansion at all airports could we make the powerful economic and environmental arguments against expansion.

require the building of a lot of new infrastructure, some in important environmental places. It would bring aircraft noise to new areas, if possibly to fewer people, as by no means all the flying could be over the sea. It would require Heathrow to be shut down or, at the very least, significantly scaled down as the market, even in South-East England, couldn't support two major international airports. Over 70,000 jobs in West London are linked to Heathrow. In theory, replacement capacity is workable. In practice, it raises many questions.

How AirportWatch functions
It is worth taking some time describing AirportWatch – what it does; how it operates, what it has achieved - because it was within the framework of AirportWatch that the historic battle to stop expansion at Heathrow took place.

AirportWatch is not an organisation in itself. It is a loose coalition of groups opposed to airport expansion. It has been supported by some of the biggest environmental organisations in the UK – Friends of the Earth, the Royal Society for the Protection of Birds, the National Trust, Greenpeace, the Woodland Trust, the World Wildlife Fund, the Campaign to Protect Rural England, the Campaign for Better Transport, Environmental Protection UK and the Aviation Environment Federation amongst them – and by bodies like the World Development Movement which are campaigning for a better deal for 'developing' countries. It also contains a wide variety of local campaign groups around airports. And these days, though not at the beginning, there are individuals who are part of it.

From the start AirportWatch saw its main role as one of co-ordination and networking. Individual organisations would do their own campaigning, lobbying and research but would be linked through the AirportWatch umbrella. AirportWatch would only carry out research and do campaigning where its supporting organisations felt there was a need for something which they were not doing. Today, it has a website – www.airportwatch.org.uk - produces information sheets, circulates a monthly bulletin, manages a Google email list, ensures an aviation presence at demonstrations, and is the first port of call for new airport community groups. Its tireless and much-loved co-ordinator, Sarah Clayton, does most of her work for free. She has a desk in the offices of the Aviation Environment Federation (AEF), the one NGO (Non-Governmental Organisation) in the UK which works exclusively on aviation. AirportWatch owes a huge amount to AEF and, in particular, to the generosity of its Director Tim Johnson and its Chair Richard Roads.

In its early days, AirportWatch had to work through some problems. This is only to be expected in any broad coalition. It took a little time to agree on some of our basic messages and exactly how we would operate. But a good number of face-to-face meetings and a growing recognition by the groups involved that we were stronger together than apart pulled us through.

I think there are a number of key things which have been fundamental to the survival and the growing success of AirportWatch:

First, we didn't get bogged down in drawing up a detailed manifesto or constitution. To do so can create division and waste time. We settled for just two things: one overall aim and one golden rule. Our aim was to get in place a demand management approach to aviation rather than the aggressive expansion favoured by the Government. We didn't define 'demand management' too closely! For some of us it meant fighting for an overall reduction in the amount of flying taking place; for others, the objective was to limit the growth in aviation. In practice, it was a difference we could all live with. Our one golden rule was that no group would suggest that the expansion should take place at somebody else's airport. It was understood that each local group would campaign hard against expansion at its own airport but that would not imply it favoured expansion elsewhere.

Second, no one issue was regarded as more important than any other. Organisations and individuals had different reasons for opposing airport expansion: climate change; climate justice for the poor world; noise; community destruction; the loss of biodiversity. Sometimes we had difficulty in fully understanding each other's issues. But AirportWatch always respected everybody's concerns and treated them all equally. Over time we all acquired a much better understanding of each other's issues.

Third, we remained very clear that we were a loose coalition, not a new organisation. We, therefore, did not threaten existing organisations. The idea was that each group would do what it was good at – lobbying; campaigning; demonstrating; research etc – but that it would then share its work with the other groups in AirportWatch. As a loose coalition, there was no one dominant organisation or person. Nobody was the public face of AirportWatch. Although I chaired AirportWatch almost from its inception, I saw my role as essentially facilitating a meeting not as a spokesperson for the network.

- **This approach had some drawbacks.** Some people found it hard to work within such a loose structure. The lack of a tight structure also meant AirportWatch struggled in its early years to deal with disruptive individuals. And, because we were not a clearly-defined organisation, we were not going to raise vast amounts of money nor achieve a high media or political profile. That didn't matter too much. Our role, as a network, was to ensure that, through the work of the organisations within AirportWatch, the profile of *the issue* was raised. We also relied on our supporting organisations for money, though we did also get some invaluable grants from green charitable bodies such as the Goldsmith-backed Manuka Trust and the mould-breaking Enough's Enough.

- **Though this form of loose association had its drawbacks, I would argue they were outweighed by its advantages.** We were able to create a movement that was diverse in its supporter base and was able to highlight all the key issues of airport expansion – economics; climate change; noise; community destruction; and the loss of biodiversity. It also meant we were able to campaign at all levels. Some organisations had well-established links with senior politicians and civil servants; others excelled at media work; one or two had a profound technical knowledge of the issues; some worked at a grassroots level; a few did radical actions. Together we came to present, I believe, a real challenge to the Government and the aviation industry. And because we were a loose association, the powers-that-be found it that much harder to pin us down. Those with power like to have the measure of any organisation opposing them; to work out what it is all about; to be able to put it in a box. That way they feel much more in control. It was to our advantage they struggled to define us. It gave *us* a measure of control.

We now know that the aviation industry and the Government never believed, in those early years, that AirportWatch would hold together. They firmly expected it would fall apart once the expansion proposals for the individual airports began to firm up. But ten years on AirportWatch is stronger than ever. It has many more supporter groups including an informal association with the direct action networks and growing links with campaign groups in Europe. Supporters exchange emails on a daily basis. We visit each other's campaigns to show support and provide advice. We attend each other's events. Many of us have become personal friends.

2. Make aviation expansion a high-profile national debate

AirportWatch set out to make airport expansion a national issue. This hadn't happened before. There had been famous individual battles, mostly lost by the campaigners, but airport expansion had never really been seen as a national concern. Aviation had rarely made it beyond the business pages of the newspapers. AirportWatch needed to make it front page news. It was an essential first step to putting the authorities under pressure. The more that aviation became to be seen as a national issue, the more difficult it would be for the Government to argue that opposition to expansion of an individual airport was merely a local matter to be dealt with at a local level. When something becomes a national issue there is more pressure from both the media and the public on the authorities to so something about it.

3. Influence that aviation debate

But we felt it had to be a new kind of debate. Flying had been seen as a good thing: good for the economy; for jobs; and for providing the chance for more and more people to travel. The only real downside mentioned was the impact of noise and air pollution on people living close to airports. None of us within AirportWatch took the view the aviation industry should shut down. But we felt it was essential that we highlight the many downsides of aviation. To do so we had to influence the debate in a number of key areas.

3a. Influence the economic debate

We started not with the environment, but with economics. We reasoned that we would make little headway unless we challenged the prevailing assumptions that airport expansion was essential for the economy. We were only too well aware that this was the ground the Government was going to flight on. In 1999 the Department for Transport had published a study by the consultants Oxford Economic Forecasting (OEF), *The Contribution of Aviation to the UK Economy*. The Government made it clear that this study was going to form the basis of its forthcoming Air Transport White Paper, the document which would set out its 30 year plan for aviation. Yet the study was hardly a neutral document. Its forward was written by leading figures in the aviation industry and it was 90% paid for by the industry. It made many questionable claims about the aviation's contribution to the economy. But the report was a coup for the industry. It had cleverly ensured the forthcoming White Paper would be based on the report. As one leading figure in the industry was to say to me some years later, "We had control of the process."

We started not with the environment, but with economics. We reasoned that we would make little headway unless we challenged the prevailing assumptions that airport expansion was essential for the economy

AirportWatch responded well. We were fortunate to have within our ranks Brendon Sewill, an economist trained at Cambridge. Brendon chairs GACC, the group campaigning against expansion at Gatwick Airport. He produced a series of well-researched but popularly written booklets which challenged many of the questionable claims within OEF report. (Some of these booklets have now been translated into French and Dutch). He showed that, far from being a net contributor to the economy, aviation was actually a drain on it. It paid no tax on its fuel. It was zero-rated for VAT. It didn't fully cover its environmental costs. Brendon calculated that the VAT rating and the tax-free fuel alone were costing the country £9 billion a year. The figure was not disputed by the Government or the aviation industry.

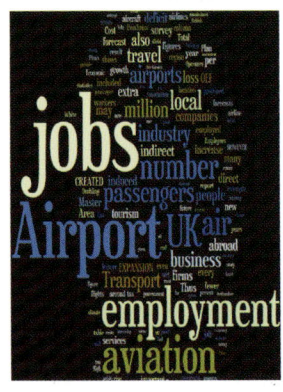

Some reports from AirportWatch have been translated into both French and Dutch.

We were making some headway. We had a memorable, accurate figure; one that challenged the prevailing thinking of the time. We repeated it time and time again. Over time, the press began to use it in their articles and politicians in their speeches. It brought home to me once again that, in the early stages of a campaign when the main aim is to change the climate of opinion, it is much more important to have a memorable figure, an eye-catching image or an attention-grabbing headline that sums up what you are all about than to worry about details of policy. They can come later.

Although it would take ten years and a new government before the Department for Transport's one-sided stance on aviation economics was finally rejected, the challenge had begun. We set up an AirportWatch economics group, chaired by Brendon Sewill, and including notable figures like Brian Ross, the economics adviser to Stop Stansted Expansion and a former businessman who had an expert grasp of economics. Over the next few years AirportWatch's work on economics was complemented by major reports from leading academics, think-tanks and respected consultancies. The industry was becoming less and less "in charge of the process."

We made progress in challenging the economic arguments

3b. Influence the climate change debate

Back in 1997 climate change was not on governments' agendas the way it was at the Copenhagen Summit in 2010. International aviation had been excluded from the Kyoto Treaty. It was becoming clear, though, that aviation was a very dirty industry indeed. Worldwide it had become the fastest-growing contributor to CO_2 emissions.

For many of the national environmental organisations within AirportWatch, climate change was *the* big concern. It was the reason they started campaigning on aviation. They saw fighting airport expansion as part of their wider campaign against the threat of climate change. Organisations such as Greenpeace and Friends of the Earth put a huge amount of resources into their climate change campaigning. A lot of Friends of the Earth's work revolved around persuading the Government to pass the Climate Change Act 2008. This was a very important milestone for all of us because the Government committed itself to clear targets to reduce CO_2 emissions. All this wider campaigning on climate change made AirportWatch's task so much easier. It underlined the value of the coalition.

Climate change was *the* big concern for many of the national organisations in AirportWatch. Photo: WDM

It was concern about climate change which also brought a lot of new campaigners, most of them under 30, into the wider environmental movement for the first time. They helped make climate campaigning what it has become today: a worldwide movement in its own right: a movement which has influence, energy and vibrancy; a movement which includes people who have forsaken careers to campaign virtually full-time; a movement where thousands have risked arrest and jail for their convictions. AirportWatch was able to tap into this vibrant new movement. AirportWatch's contribution was to highlight the impact airport expansion would have on climate. Over time, our work helped embed in the minds of the public, politicians and the media that aggressive aviation expansion was not compatible with serious action to tackle climate change.

> **Climate change campaigning has become a worldwide movement which has influence, energy and vibrancy; a movement which includes people who have forsaken careers to campaign virtually full-time; a movement where thousands have risked arrest and jail for their convictions. AirportWatch tapped into this.**

3c. Influence the climate justice debate

In its early years AirportWatch regularly faced the charge that it was 'trying to stop poor people flying'. We were accused, when we campaigned for an end to subsidies, that it would stop hard-working families from taking their annual holiday on the beaches of Spain as fares would have to go up. It would have been a big drawback if a charge like that had stuck. We would have been seen as elitist. We worked hard to counter the argument. We showed that the proposed expansion was driven by the wealthiest 10% of the population who flew abroad five or six times a year. We pointed out the amount of extra tax hard-working families paid each year to make up for the money lost through the tax-breaks the aviation industry received was over £500. Slowly we began to get across the fact that the argument was more complex than our detractors made out. The strongest argument we had, though, in refuting our critics, centred around climate justice. We highlighted the fact that it was the poorest people in the poor world, those least likely of any on earth to fly, who were the real victims of rich countries' aggressive airport expansion plans as climate change would hit them first and most acutely. That was the real inequity. AirportWatch's credibility was greatly enhanced when organisations like the World Development Movement and Christian Aid became associated with us.

We had to counter the argument that we were trying to stop poor people flying

3d. Influence the noise debate

Photo: Weedon

Noise was the main concern of most of the local airport campaign groups. The aviation industry and the Department for Transport argued noise was becoming less of a problem because individual planes had become significantly quieter over the past 30 years. It was true that the planes had become quieter but that had been off-set by the huge growth in the number of planes. It was this sheer volume of aircraft that had become such a problem. AirportWatch's task was to get across that, in reality, the noise climate had got a lot worse. This was made more difficult by the way the official figures were (and are) compiled. Noise is averaged over a year - which doesn't reflect accurately the disturbance of a plane as it passes over. Indeed, many in authority do not seem to understand noise. A senior BAA manager said to me shortly after I started campaigning: "I never knew that noise at Heathrow was a real problem. I thought that the people were just using it as an excuse because they didn't approve of the airport." I'm not sure that AirportWatch has succeeded yet in getting across to decision-makers and the wider public how debilitating aircraft noise can be for some people. In part this may be because only a minority of noise campaigners have shown the same urgency and vibrancy which has characterised the climate change movement, despite so many local people in the campaign groups being deeply affected by aircraft noise. Unlike climate change, there is no worldwide movement for peace and quiet. Perhaps this is because noise is seen as a local and individual problem, however widespread it *actually* is. Noise affects more people in their day-to-day lives than any other pollutant. From New York to Rio de Janerio, noise tops the list of complaints received by the local authorities. Yet the movement is absent.

Only a minority of noise campaigners have shown the urgency and vibrancy which has characterised the climate change movement

The UK Noise Association

The UK Noise Association (UKNA) was set up in 2000. It was the brainchild of Val Weedon, the leading anti-noise campaigner of her generation in the UK. It brought together organisations concerned about all different aspects of noise. Its purpose was to put noise as an issue up the political agenda. It has been a frustrating struggle. The Labour Government showed no interest in noise. UKNA is hoping for more progress with the new Government.

4. Build links with Europe

AirportWatch set out to develop closer links with lobby groups and campaigners in Europe. We felt this was essential for two main reasons. One, many decisions about the direction of aviation policy are being taken at a European level. We had to try and counter the powerful lobbying presence the aviation industry had in Europe. Two, the links would enable groups to learn from and support each other. These links with Europe have taken two basic forms. The national environmental organisations have joined forces to lobby European decision-makers working alongside Brussels-based lobby groups such as Transport and Environment and the European Environmental Bureau. They have built on work done in the 1990s by the likes of 'The Right Price for Air Travel' campaign, based in the Netherlands. At the same time, the grassroots airport campaign groups have made links with their fellow campaign groups in Europe, often through UECNA, the Europe-wide body of grassroots organisations.

5. Expose the bias of the civil servants

The stance of the civil servants in the Department for Transport's (DfT) aviation division has been a big factor in the way aviation policy has developed. These are the people who have been advising government as it put together its policy, who have been whispering in the ears of a succession of aviation ministers. And yet their position has been far from neutral. It became clear during the Heathrow campaign just how close the DfT civil servants were to the aviation industry. The Sunday Times published leaked documents which revealed 'collusion' between them and BAA. And a number of senior civil servants have taken top jobs in the aviation industry. David Rowlands, the Permanent Secretary at the DfT, i.e. its most senior civil servant, is now Chairman of the company running Gatwick Airport. Roy Griffins, the civil servant in charge of producing the 2003 Air Transport White Paper, now is the Director General of the Airports Council International (Europe). I don't believe these civil servants are taking backhanders from the aviation industry; simply that they see their main role as creating the right conditions for the UK aviation industry to flourish economically, other considerations very much taking second place. If that is their mind-set, their closeness to the industry should not come as a surprise. The rest of us, to a greater or lesser extent, simply are not very useful to them and tend to get in the way.

> Chris Mullin, in his short time as Aviation Minister, tried to get something done on a related issue: night flights. His diaries are very revealing about the attitude of the civil servants:
>
> *"Wednesday 14th June....the much-postponed meeting between the MPs for Putney and Windsor and representatives of the airlines to discuss the night flights...officials have done all in their power to discourage action, but I persisted....*
>
> *Thursday 9th November...Another meeting, against official advice, with Putney MP Tony Colman about night flights...needless to say nothing has happened. Our official who sat in on the meeting made no secret of his view that nothing can be done and deeply resents my meddling...the relationship between the airlines and the Department is far too cosy"*

New Aviation Minister Theresa Villiers is ushering in a new approach at the DfT

I know there are many decent civil servants in the DfT. I know, too, that some people left the DfT because they couldn't stomach its dodgy dealings over Heathrow. And I sense some who stayed are relieved that Heathrow expansion has been scrapped and that the new Government is developing a very different aviation policy to the one of aggressive expansion pursued under Labour. But there is no doubt that the civil service was a major problem for us. There are though signs things could be changing. Theresa Villiers, the Minister responsible for aviation in the new Government, is ushering in a new approach. She recognises that the expansionist policies of the previous government are not viable. In opposition she had played a key role in ensuring the Conservatives opposed further expansion at Heathrow.

The Heathrow Campaign

I began to chair HACAN, the Heathrow residents' organisation, in 2000. I had first become involved in aviation campaigning two or three years earlier. What prompted me was the sudden problem of aircraft noise over my house. I had lived and worked in South London for twenty years. Aircraft noise had never been a problem. I had always seen it as something of concern in West London and Windsor. That all changed in the second half of the 1990s. Aircraft started roaring overhead, sometimes at a rate of one every 90 seconds. I was not alone. Disparate individuals came together. We held public meetings, one attended by the local MP Kate Hoey, who has been a firm supporter of the campaign ever since. We formed an organisation called ClearSkies. The Department for Transport, with an evasiveness we were to come to know so well, said that nothing had changed and that, anyway, we were far too far from Heathrow for noise to be a problem. (We subsequently learnt significant changes *had* been made). More than a dozen years later, aircraft noise is still a problem in South London. We may have stopped a third runway but the daily turmoil for people who never expected to be under a flight path goes on.

A feature of the last 15 years has been the way in which aircraft noise has become a problem many miles from Heathrow.
Photo: Weedon

Despite the noise overhead, I thought long and hard about getting involved in a campaign. I had been campaigning against road building schemes in London and then, nationally, for more than a decade. I suspected it would be another decade before we saw any success in the airport campaign. I wasn't sure I wanted to take on such a big task. I disappeared to Scotland to think about it. I couldn't decide what to do. But once back in London, with the planes waking me before 6am every morning, I knew I had no choice. Many people are not disturbed by even relatively high levels of aircraft noise, but for those who are, planes become a constant intrusion in their lives. In 2000 ClearSkies, merged with HACAN, the organisation which had been based in West London for many decades, to become HACAN ClearSkies. What one journalist (quite rightly) called the world's worst name! HACAN had had some successes. In the 1970s it persuaded the authorities to introduce 'runway alternation' - this requires planes landing over West London to switch runways at 3pm in order to allow people in the boroughs close to Heathrow a half day's break from the noise. Working alongside FANG (the Federation of Airport Noise Groups), it had fought hard to keep the restrictions on night flights. Under the leadership of my impressive predecessor, Dermot Cox, HACAN persuaded the Terminal 5 Inspector to recommend a cap of 480,000 a year on the number of flights using the airport. This was to turn out to be critical. But, generally, expansion had gone unchecked. The authorities promised each major expansion would be the last. But every promise was broken. In the 1990s during the Terminal Five Public Enquiry, lasting over 3 years, the longest in British history, Sir John Egan, the Chief Executive of BAA, the company which owns Heathrow, wrote to local people saying BAA would not call for a third runway. Yet by 2002, the Government was consulting on proposals for airport expansion across the UK, including plans for a third runway and a sixth terminal at Heathrow.

Dermot Cox, my impressive predecessor as chair of HACAN, who won the critical concession that the number of flights at Heathrow would be capped.

> **Over the years the Heathrow campaigners had had some successes but generally it was a story of the authorities getting their way.**

The Need to Learn from Past Failures

As we drew up our strategy to combat the threat of expansion, we were determined to learn the lessons of past failures.

There were three main lessons to be learnt.

First we had been too small and lacked enough clout to win our past battles. We needed to build a coalition. Even with the support of some local authorities, a number of MPs and some local environmental groups, we had not been strong enough to win, however good many of our arguments had been. This time we needed to build as diverse and powerful a coalition as possible. Good arguments alone rarely win campaigns.

Secondly, we needed to challenge the economic justification given for expansion. In the past, with the local authorities and local environmental organisations such as West London Friends of the Earth, we had opposed expansion on environmental grounds – largely noise and air pollution – but had not challenged the Government and industry's central argument: expansion was needed for economic reasons. We had fought with one hand behind our backs.

Thirdly, we needed to set the agenda. We couldn't just rely on making objections during the public consultation and appearing at the public inquiry. To be fair to it, the Terminal 5 campaign was more than that, but the Public Inquiry became a central feature. Reliance on public inquiries and public consultations has rarely been successful. If objectors were to win regularly using these forums, the Government would soon abolish them! The powers-that-be 'sell' these procedures very well, using the words 'public' and 'consultation' as often as possible. It is no wonder that people fall for them; that ordinary citizens believe these are the places where they can have their say and influence matters. In reality, these procedures have been carefully designed to allow governments and businesses to get their pet schemes through. Only one national road scheme, for example – the Hereford Bypass in the mid-1990s – has ever been stopped at a public inquiry. Although a handful of regional and local road schemes have been dropped at public inquiries as have some plans for airport expansion, the clear message is: don't put your faith in public consultations or public inquiries! Particularly for a project as big as a third runway. We need to do it for ourselves. That means pro-active campaigning. It means setting the agenda; campaigning long before a public inquiry is even a gleam in an Inspector's eye; stirring things up in our communities; sounding out our politicians; cultivating the media; only using public consultations if they are useful to us. It also, in my opinion, means direct action.

> **Reliance on public inquiries and public consultations has rarely been successful.**

> **We needed to do it for ourselves through pro-active, agenda-setting campaigning.**

What we were facing

- **A big increase of planes on the existing runways**
- **A third runway and 6th terminal**
- **Total flight numbers to rise to over 700,000 a year**
- **At least 150,000 people under the new flight path**
- **Over 1 million people disturbed by noise from Heathrow**
- **At least 700 homes destroyed**
- **Air Pollution set to exceed the EU legal limits**
- **Heathrow set to become the single biggest source of CO_2 in the UK**

Direct Action

Direct action is always controversial.

Most people aren't instinctively comfortable with breaking the law. Except when we are driving…. and speeding! Or maybe filling in tax returns? Or going through the amber light as it turns to red? Most of us actually do break the law. Quite often! And usually in more dangerous ways than demonstrating on the roof of the House of Commons or even occupying a taxiway at East Midlands Airport. But, however illogical it may be, many campaigners don't go for direct action!

My own view is that direct action is an important part of the mix if we are fighting to achieve radical change against the odds - like trying to defeat a proposal as important to the authorities as the third runway. History shows that direct action or civil disobedience has played a proven role in the great struggles of the past, from the Suffragettes to the American civil rights movement, Stopping Heathrow expansion may or may not be in the same league as those struggles (though the fight to prevent runaway climate change almost certainly is) but there was no doubt in my mind that to win our battle against a third runway direct action would need to be part of the package.

My own view is that direct action is an important part of the mix if we are fighting to achieve radical change against the odds - like trying to defeat a proposal as important to the authorities as the third runway.

My own involvement in direct action came from the days of the so-called 'anti-roads' movement in the 1990s. I had helped set up and chaired ALARM UK, the umbrella body of over 250 local community groups opposing road schemes across the country. We worked closely with Road Alert, the network of activists who took direct action at places such as Twyford Down, Newbury and the M11 Link Road in East London.

That movement was spectacularly successful. Of the 600 schemes proposed in the 1989 road building programme, by 1997 only 150 remained. Some had been built but the majority had been abandoned. Direct action was not the sole reason for the success. It was down to a mix of solid community campaigning, the sound economic and environmental arguments made by academics and national environmental organisations as well as persistent direct action. Nobody will ever know whether we would have won without the direct action but I feel it played an important role: as well as dramatising the issue, it put real pressure on the Government and frightened the construction industry in a way that conventional campaigning on its could not have done.

I felt direct action, for exactly those reasons, needed to be part of the Heathrow campaign. However, it became clear that it could not be part of HACAN's agenda. Although a minority of our members strongly favoured direct action, the majority decided HACAN should not be an organisation associated with direct action.

I will return to the direct action story.

2002: The Heathrow Campaign Begins

What was to become an iconic campaign began in 2002 when the proposals for a third runway and sixth terminal first emerged in a government consultation. We set out on our long march to stop expansion at Heathrow.

2003 Air Transport White Paper

In 2003 the Air Transport White Paper was published. It contained proposals for the biggest single programme of airport expansion this country had ever faced. It expected a trebling in passengers using UK airports by 2030 and envisaged new runways in the South East, at Heathrow and Stansted, with Gatwick as a fall-back; a possible new runway at Birmingham; one or two new runways in Scotland; plus "full use" of existing runways at most other airports. For Heathrow, there was an added sting in the tail. There was a proposal to abolish 'runway alternation', the practice where planes landing over West London switch runways at 3pm to give residents in the places close to the airport a break from the noise. That had not been part of the consultation. The one, rather perverse, advantage of the White Paper was that it envisaged so much expansion it provided a very clear focus for AirportWatch groups to unite around.

We faced the biggest single expansion plan ever.

2003 and 2004: Difficult Years

However, 2003 and 2004 were difficult years. HACAN had just lost its case at the European Court of Human Rights to ban the hated night flights. The legal challenge to the White Paper had failed. And I suppose I had doubts in my own mind just how strongly the majority of people in West London (and on the other side of the airport in Berkshire) were committed to fighting the expansion proposals. Climate change wasn't a big issue in the area and I began to wonder whether West London, an area I hardly knew prior to the campaign, had come to terms with the noise and was resigned to it. People were angry at decades of broken promises and many individuals gave generously of their time and money but were only a minority angry enough and fearful enough for the future to have the vigour to give their all to defeat the expansion proposals? I didn't know and I'm still not sure. It may be that the struggle against Terminal Five had left people disillusioned and tired.

I had doubts just how strongly the majority of people of West London were committed to fighting to the expansion

I wanted us to go in harder, not just about the third runway but also about the existing noise climate people had to endure. Some people felt we were being too timid. I knew they were right but, in any campaign, you have got to take the bulk of your supporters with you. I can think of one young man in North London who was experiencing aircraft noise for the first time. He worked hard for HACAN, but then left, disillusioned. He's now probably moved house. We failed him. And others like him.

All campaigners at their low points wonder whether it is worth carrying on. It nearly always is! The authorities want us to lose heart and give up. So often their strategy is to sit it out until we can fight on no longer. Only if you have lost, and clearly lost, is it maybe time to give up. If it is still yours to win, keep going! What helps enormously in difficult times is being able to share thoughts and feelings with fellow campaigners. This is easiest done if we know them well – a key reasons why campaigning should be about more than just formal meetings. I never really thought of giving up. We had devised a good strategy: to build a coalition, challenge the economic need for a third runway, and set the agenda. My doubts were around whether we could deliver it, given the lukewarm support in many local areas. It made me more convinced than ever that we needed the coalition.

All campaigners at times want to give up. Often the authorities' strategy is to sit it out wait until we lose heart.

The Coalition Takes Shape

The coalition started to come together.

1. Cross-Party group of politicians

We got together a cross-party group of MPs who were against expansion at Heathrow. It was chaired by John McDonnell, the Labour MP for Hayes and Harlington, who had opposed expansion at Heathrow for over 20 years. His constituency included both Heathrow Airport and the 700 or so homes which were under threat of demolition to make way for the third runway and sixth terminal.

The cross-party group included new Conservative MPs with constituencies under the flight paths like Justine Greening and Adam Afyrie; John Randall, the Conservative MP for Uxbridge whose constituency bordered John McDonnell's; Nick Hurd, the Conservative MP for Ruislip; leading Liberal Democrats like Susan Kramer, Vincent Cable, and Tom Brake; mainstream Labour MPs Alan and Ann Keen; and sympathetic peers such Lord Richard Faulkner, Baronesses Sally Hamwee, Sarah Ludford and Jenny Tonge (HACAN's President).

The cross-party group became an important part of the coalition. The MPs and peers backed each other up in parliamentary debates.

HACAN acted as the Secretariat for the group. The cross-party group was to become an important part of the coalition. Regardless of political affiliation, the MPs backed each other up in debates about Heathrow in Parliament. They put down parliamentary questions and initiated early day motions. Together they used the machinery of government to highlight the Heathrow issues in the Parliamentary arena. The key to the group's success was it members' ability to mostly set aside their other differences to present a united front on Heathrow. We subsequently learnt that the Department for Transport expected the cross-party group, which was also attended by local authority representatives, Greater London Authority members and campaigners, to dissolve in acrimony. Instead, it became a key part of the campaign.

John McDonnell MP, Chair of the Cross-Group Party Group

> John McDonnell was a key figure in the campaign. He was very much on the left of the Labour Party. He chaired the Campaign Group, the group of left-wing Labour MPs in Parliament. He voted against the New Labour Government more times than just about any other Labour MP. But his manner was consensual. He chaired the cross-party group in an inclusive manner. He helped give it strategic direction. John was also important at a constituency level. He has superb organisation skills. Within days of an important announcement on Heathrow his office would have dropped a leaflet through the doors of his constituency and a Public Meeting would take place.
>
> **John McDonnell was a pivotal figure in our campaign; a giant of the movement; his dedication to the cause was remarkable.**
>
> He understood the importance of campaigning and organising at all levels, from parliamentary to direct action. He publicly supported the direct action activists. He embraced the emerging ideas and new movements around climate change.
>
> His sheer dedication to the cause was remarkable. Whether it was giving up a Saturday to be at a day-long conference organised by campaigners, attending the local group's Carol Service on a Sunday evening, pitching his tent amongst the activists at Climate Camp or regularly rushing back from Parliament to take part in a demonstration at Heathrow, John was there.
>
> I tend to think that campaigns are won by movements rather than individuals, and I certainly know John does, but individuals can be important in shaping the direction of any campaign. John McDonnell was a pivotal figure in our campaign; a giant of the movement.

Who was who in the cross-party group

The cross-party group didn't have members. It had a mailing list of MPs and peers who were known to be opposed to the Heathrow expansion proposals and who were active in fighting them. The list below is not a comprehensive one but gives a flavour of the group:

John McDonnell MP, Labour, Chair of the group

John Randall MP, a Conservative Whip, a committed environmentalist, regularly spoke at meetings, rallies and initiated debates in Parliament

Adam Afyrie MP, new Conservative MP, active in Parliament; attended a number of rallies and meetings

Nick Hurd MP, Conservative, vocal on climate change issues

Justine Greening MP, another new Conservative MP, became a major player in the campaign

Jenny Tonge

Adam Afyrie

Theresa May MP, Conservative frontbench spokeswoman, on-side

Susan Kramer MP, very active, attended most of the coalition's events, headed up the Liberal Democrat opposition to expansion

Vincent Cable MP, deputy leader of the Liberal Democrats and their renowned economics spokesman, regularly attended rallies and meetings

Tom Brake MP, Liberal Democrat spokesman on London, active in Parliament

Alan Keen MP, mainstream Labour MP, played an important role in lobbying his Labour colleagues

Ann Keen MP, Labour Spokeswoman on Health, former Parliamentary Private Secretary to Gordon Brown

Kate Hoey MP, former Minister for Sport, a supporter for over a decade

Joan Ruddock MP, became Climate Change Minister, helpful to campaigners on a range of Heathrow issues

Lord Richard Faulkner, a Labour peer, strong supporter who regularly raised the issue in the Lords

Sarah Ludford and Vincent Cable

Baroness Sally Hamwee, Liberal Democrat peer and former GLA member, a quietly effective opponent of Heathrow expansion over many years

John Randall

Baroness Jenny Tonge, former Lib Dem MP now in the Lords; staunch supporter over many years; now HACAN President

Baroness Sarah Ludford, Lib Dem MEP for London, regular speaker at rallies

Darren Johnson, Green Chair of the GLA Environment Committee which conducted useful investigations into Heathrow expansion

Jenny Jones, Green GLA member, a regular attendee at marches and rallies

Murad Qureshi, Labour GLA member, succeeded Darren Johnson as Chair of the Environment Committee; regular attendee at marches, rallies and meetings

Richard Barnes, Conservative GLA member, became Deputy Mayor, long-time supporter

Tony Arbour, Conservative GLA member, effective Chair of its Economic Committee, which exposed flaws in the expansion plans.

2. The Mayor of London and the London Assembly

HACAN also lobbied the then Mayor of London Ken Livingstone and the London Assembly. The Mayor had helped us with our European night flights case and was again supportive in the battle against Heathrow expansion. We also successfully lobbied the London Assembly. We got cross-party support with the exception of one of the very small parties, Veritas. But this comprehensive level of support didn't come overnight. It was the result of a lot of lobbying of individual assembly members. Neither the Mayor nor the Assembly had any power over Heathrow. Both, though, represented important voices of elected representatives. The Assembly had a number of committees which carried out investigations into a range of subjects. These proved very useful to us. Both the Environment Committee and the Economic Committee conducted investigations into Heathrow expansion which showed up the many flaws in the Government's proposals.

Labour's Murad Qureshi, one of the many London Assembly members who supported us

In the 2008 Mayoral Elections, we persuaded the candidates from all four main parties to oppose expansion at Heathrow – Conservatives, Labour, Liberal Democrats and Greens. Generous funding from Enough's Enough and Greenpeace enabled us to take out a full-page advert in the London Evening Standard highlighting the opposition of the candidates. This captured the headlines big-time. This level of publicity would not have been possible if we had not been part of a wider coalition.

3. The local authorities

For some years we had worked with key local authorities. Four of them (Wandsworth, Richmond, Hillingdon and Hounslow) came together to oppose expansion under the name of 2M (representing together 2 million people under the flight paths). Many more were persuaded to come on board after an early rally staged by the No Third Runway Action Group (NoTRAG) and HACAN where council leaders saw the strength of feeling there was against expansion. By the end of the campaign, 26 local authorities across London and the Home Counties had joined. Much of the behind-the-scenes work by the local authority officers and politicians, using their contacts, was vital to our success. There is much more to be written about this. The support of the many of the local authorities and members of the Greater London Assembly hadn't, though, been automatic. It was the result of a lot of our time spent lobbying them. In this we were often assisted by already on-board councillors like Ruth Cadbury, the deputy leader of the Labour group on Hounslow Council in West London as well as established figures like Wansdworth Council leader, the Conservative Edward Lister and Serge Lourie, the Liberal Democrat leader of Richmond.

Many of the local authority officers were quiet heroes of the campaign. Their diligent, detailed work behind-the-scenes provided us all with solid information.

Labour Councillor Ruth Cadbury, a long-time and hard-working supporter

4. Greenpeace and the environmental groups

The next big entrant was Greenpeace. For some time I had been having discussions with them as they went through the process of deciding whether to make Heathrow one of their big priority campaigns. With hindsight, their decision to do so was one of the most important things that happened to the campaign. Their contribution has been immense. Greenpeace provided a wealth of radical campaigning experience, high-quality media expertise, an abundance of ideas and valuable resources. But perhaps most impressive of all, under its Director John Sauven, it sought not to dominate the coalition but simply to contribute to the growing social movement that this campaign was to become.

Photo: Greenpeace

Greenpeace's contribution to the campaign was huge

It brought not only its famed direct action but also:

- a wealth of radical campaigning experience
- high-quality, professional media expertise
- an abundance of ideas
- and valuable resources.

Many other national organisations came on board:

- The World Wildlife Fund
- The National Trust
- The Campaign Against Climate Change
- Enough's Enough
- The Society for the Protection of Ancient Buildings
- The World Development Movement
- West London Friends of The Earth
- The Campaign to Protect Rural England
- The Royal Society for the Protection of Birds
- The Campaign for Better Transport
- The Aviation Environment Federation

Anna Jones and colleagues from Greenpeace played a critical role in the coalition.
Photo: Greenpeace

Pete Lockley played a crucial role in the campaign when working at both AEF and WWF. He combined a radical approach with a clear grasp of the details of climate change and aviation.

5. The No Third Runway Action Group

The story of NoTRAG is the story of the human spirit defying all odds. Ordinary women who fought their way through exhaustion and traumas to do extraordinary things

NoTRAG Chair Geraldine Nicholson and Secretary Linda McCutcheon and local historian Philip Sherwood greet London Mayor Ken Livingston in Sipson

NoTRAG. The No Third Runway Action Group. Our sister organisation, it represented the people with most to lose if a third runway was built: their homes and their communities. The village of Sipson would have been wiped off the map, with the destruction of at least 700 homes. The surrounding areas of Harmondsworth, Harlington and West Drayton might have been even worse off: they would have been left with a new runway and a terminal on their doorstep. NoTRAG had been going since 2002 when plans for a third runway and sixth terminal first emerged. It had organised marches and demonstrations. Its first Chair Gill Cannon had done a tremendous job of welding together people traumatised by the threat to their communities and homes into an effective campaigning body. But NoTRAG really sprang to life one remarkable evening in 2005. BAA had just published detailed plans showing for the first time the land and homes which would be required for the new

NoTRAG represented the people with most to lose if a third runway was built: their homes and their communities

runway and terminal. NoTRAG called a meeting in Heathrow Primary School, the award-winning local school which stood in the line of a third runway. Well over a thousand people turned up. The hall was packed. It was standing room only….in the playground outside. I spoke as did the MPs John McDonnell and John Randall but the star of the evening was the new Chair of NoTRAG, Geraldine Nicholson. Passionate, funny, with all the local detail at her fingertips, she had the crowd on its feet. This is not the sort of oratory they can teach you in formal lessons on public speaking. These words flowed from the heart: a mother of three fighting to save the school her young boys went to; fighting for the community she grew up in, the pub, the church, the village shop. Fighting to stop the forced removal of thousands of people; her friends and neighbours. One meeting wasn't enough. For the next five nights we spoke at different village halls, each of them packed. This was a community in revolt.

1,000 people packed a public meeting. This was a community in revolt.

A Community Facing Wipe Out

It is hard to imagine a community of 3,000 people being wiped off the face of the earth. The houses, the schools, the shops, the pubs, the churches, all gone. That's what would have happened to Sipson. It was unreal and eerie to walk around the village and realise it could all be under concrete. Sipson, like the surrounding villages and nearby West Drayton were not rich communities. But they were pleasant places to live. Although close to Heathrow, they are not overflown as they are parallel to the airport. And the villages have a proud history, particularly Harmondsworth. It has a village square, a parish church dating back to the 11th century and the oldest remaining tithe barn in the country. The threatened King William 1V pub in Sipson is 16th century. The villages first faced extinction shortly after the airport was built in the 1940s but the Government's Air Transport Committee in the early 1950s ruled out demolishing them as "No Government would be prepared to consider a project that involved razing the three old-world villages of Harmondsworth, Sipson and Harlington to the ground (1)." How times change!

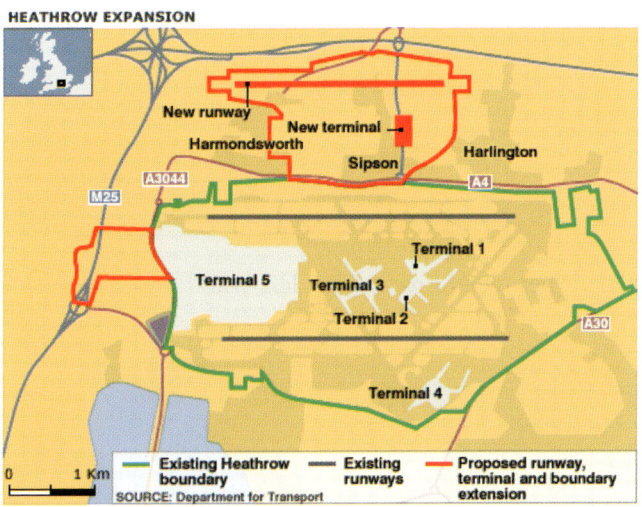

Photo: Weedon

People Living on the Edge

What the people in NoTRAG brought to the coalition was immeasurable. Every campaign needs stories of real people. Stories that people sitting in front of their televisions at home can instantly relate to. NoTRAG had them in abundance.

Geraldine Nicholson, the long-time Chair of NoTRAG. Geraldine grew up in the area. Her home in West Drayton would have been 100 yards from the new runway. Geraldine is a single mother of three young boys.

Linda McCutcheon, NoTRAG Secretary, had lived in Sipson for over 40 years, all her married life. She had wed Terry, a local boy, in the church down the road. Her children were christened and went to school in the area. Her elderly mother lived across the road. She looked after her home and garden with tender care. All would go, buried under the tarmac of a third runway and sixth terminal. **Photo: Pushinsky**

Christine Taylor, the NoTRAG Vice Chair, had worked at the BBC but now she was bringing up her boys in home territory. Her elderly mother had lived within sight of the airport all her life but had not flown until 2009. And then just to Manchester to see what it was like! **Photo: Pushinsky**

Audrey had lived in the area 80 years. She was now widowed. In her youth she had represented London in the athletic championships at the White City Stadium but all her life had centred around Harmondsworth, Sipson and Harlington. She would have ended her days living beside a new terminal. (She's pictured with Gabriel from Plane Stupid). **Photo: Pushinsky**

Ann and Bryan Sobey (right) had chaired the residents association for 50 years. Bryan had come from the West Country to work at the airport. For Bryan and Ann, the area was a labour of love. Ann died in Sipson two years before the campaign was won.

Christine Shilling, in Harmondsworth for 40 years. NoTRAG Press Secretary, a retired Senior Educational Psychologist who became a key contact with the faith communities.

There were more people besides, too many to name, people like:

Tracy who worked in the local King William 1V pub in Sipson, a mum with two children, the life and soul of every party, gave her all for the campaign. Tracy is pictured in action later in the book.

Armelle Thomas and **Eilish Stone** who fought so hard to save Harmondsworth, also pictured later.

NoTRAG would be joined in due course by a campaign to save a local cemetery, Cherry Lane, part of which was under threat from a new road needed to access the new runway and terminal. Another campaign headed up by remarkable women, people like **Natasha and Edna La Mothe and Linda Gritt**

But NoTRAG provided much more than good human interest stories to the coalition. These were not people who ever expected they would need to take on the might of government and the aviation industry. These were ordinary hard-working people whose lives were being turned upside down; who couldn't plan for the future; whose homes and communities were under an ever-present threat. If their homes were demolished, they would get some compensation. If they were left on the edge of a runway, no compensation.

The story of NoTRAG became the story of the human spirit defying all the odds. The women of the area – and it was largely a women-led campaign – despite children to look after, and homes to tend, and elderly parents to care for, and jobs to hold down, fought their way through exhaustion and often deeply personal traumas to do things they never saw themselves doing and go places they never imagined they would find themselves in. They addressed crowds of thousands. They were on platforms at party conferences. They became

NoTRAG Chair Geraldine Nicholson addressing a fringe meeting at the Labour Party Conference

regulars on television and in the newspapers. They dug for victory alongside direct action campaigners. They invaded prestigious conferences and receptions. They defiantly danced inside Heathrow Airport! And all the time they produced sound, solid arguments as to why the destruction they were facing was utterly unnecessary. There were difficulties and tensions as there would be in any community fighting for its survival; living on the edge. Towards the end some residents of Sipson,

The women of the area went places they never imagined they would go: to party conferences; television studios: addressing crowds of thousands.

after years trapped by blight, accepted offers from BAA for their houses. But sheer determination to preserve their community, and, in the end, an unshakeable belief they could win, saw them through. There is much more to be written about the community that defied the odds. Words which will inspire battling communities everywhere. But, if NoTRAG brought so much to the coalition, being part of the coalition helped NoTRAG. It brought them into contact with experienced campaigners. It made it easier for them to get a national platform. It ensured they weren't on their own. NoTRAG won as part of the coalition.

3:07 There is much still to be written about the community that defied the odds. Words which will inspire battling communities everywhere. Hear about the campaign in Linda's own words: http://www.youtube.com/watch?v=KZZ_ZNr7vO8

HACAN'S Role in the Coalition

HACAN is a very different organisation from NoTRAG. We have been around a long time, since the late 1960s. We started as KACAN, a residents group in the wealthy West London areas of Kew and Richmond. By the mid-1980s, HACAN's membership had expanded to include people across West London and Berkshire. At the start of the campaign against the third runway in 2000 we had several thousand members scattered all over London and the Home Counties. This reflected the way in which aircraft noise had spread over the years.

Noise the main concern

Noise, the incessant roar of the planes overhead, is the main concern of most HACAN members. Its name reflects that – Heathrow Association fir the Control of Aircraft Noise. It is a diverse organisation with members from all income groups. Probably around 5 – 7% of its membership is from ethnic minority backgrounds. It doesn't have many members under 30. Nor do many people who have recently moved into a property under the flight path join. They tend to be aware of the current noise situation and have factored it into the equation when they move in. The members tend to fall into two broad groups: those who have lived under the flight path for many years, but never expected the noise climate to get as bad as it is today, particularly given the repeated promises by the Government and the aviation industry that expansion would come to an end; and those many miles from the airport who moved into their properties when aircraft noise was not an issue in their areas. It only became a problem when the Government allowed alterations to the flight paths in order to cater for the increased number of planes using the airport. The aircraft noise came to these people; they did not move to the noise.

The very real impact of noise on ordinary people played an important role in persuading politicians that expansion was unacceptable

The expansion proposals brought two big concerns for HACAN members. Traditional HACAN territory – people living in boroughs like Richmond and Hounslow – benefitted from runway alternation, the practice where aircraft landing over London switch runways at 3pm to give people a half day's break from the noise. The Government's plans to abolish this were a major worry. The other concern was the extra planes which a third runway would bring.

Campaigning outside its comfort zone

Monica Robb and Jim Davidson, two of the unsung heroes of the campaign

HACAN had a tradition of campaigning in a fairly conventional way. The more radical approach adopted in this campaign took it out of its comfort zone. As the new Chair, but coming from a different background, I had to be aware of this. But there was virtually no active resistance to the new approach. Because so many members had had their eyes opened by the dirty tricks used against them in the past they were willing for the organisation to campaign in a more pro-active style. But most HACAN members were not active in the way the women of NoTRAG were, although many gave very generously to enable us to campaign. But, if I'm honest, I found this lack of involvement frustrating. I know the frustration was shared by a number of the more active members in the organisation. Having said that I was constantly amazed and humbled at the amount of work very many people did for no reward. The campaign owes these unsung heroes a huge debt. HACAN's strength is that it is made up of real people with real concerns.

Most people have not joined it for political or ideological reasons. They have been driven to sign up by the constant intrusion of aircraft noise in their lives. That in itself sends a powerful message to politicians. The very real impact of noise on ordinary people played an important role in persuading politicians that expansion was unacceptable. However, the strengths of HACAN –

people's real concerns about the problem in their own community - can also mean it has struggled to be excited by the bigger picture. We got there in the end. Our members were proud to be part of a famous victory and most understood the value of the wider coalition.

HACAN becomes the driver of the coalition

Around 2000 HACAN decided that, if we were to mount a serious campaign, it needed to employ somebody. So I became paid. I think we took the view that HACAN was probably ideally placed to bring together the coalition and to service it. Along with NoTRAG we were the only organisation which focused entirely on Heathrow. Local authorities, MPs, environmental organisations had interests and responsibilities in addition to Heathrow. HACAN, therefore, became the natural hub and driver of the coalition.

Funding

People are curious as to where our funding came from. Part of the value of a coalition is that resources can be shared.

HACAN is funded through subscriptions and donations from its members. We get the occasional grant to fund a particular project, such as the money from the Ashden Trust which helped pay for our economics report. For the two years either side of the consultation our income shot up. This was partly as a result of increased publicity but it was also down to two generous grants from the Goldsmith Trusts, one a direct grant, the other income from an extraordinary cricket match. When I had met with Zac Goldsmith, he suggested organising a benefit cricket match for HACAN. It was no ordinary match! Imran Khan, the former captain of Pakistan, captained one team; the world-famous Australian spin bowler, Shane Warne, the other. It raised £20,000. A great boost for HACAN. A surreal Saturday afternoon on Ham Common in West London. And the sort of event the media love.

Ray Puddifoot, the long-time leader of Hillingdon Council, which generously funded NoTRAG and part of the 2M group which put a lot of resources into the court case.

NoTRAG gets most of its money from the London Borough of Hillingdon, the borough where the majority of its members live.

Greenpeace and the other national environmental organisations brought their resources – the result of the huge number of individual supporters they have.

The local authorities often provided help in kind – the use of town halls etc for meetings – and were generous in funding to a large extent some of the court cases.

The Heathrow Coalition – and AirportWatch – also received generous support from Enough's Enough, three businessmen who were now devoting a lot of their time and money to fighting climate change.

Zac Goldsmith, who organised the charity cricket match in aid of HACAN, was much more than a generous donor to the campaign. The former editor of the Ecologist, he had a deep understanding of the environmental damage that Heathrow expansion would cause. Within the Conservative Party, he became a strong advocate of the green policies espoused by its new leader David Cameron. He also played an important role in debunking the argument that a third runway was essential for the health of the economy.

Plane Stupid is Born

So the coalition was taking shape, but I was still looking for direct action activists. I made contact with old friends from the anti-roads movement. I visited them in different parts of the country. But they were doing other things. There had been some direct action at Heathrow. Five activists spent a week on top of a crane on the site of Terminal 5. I had been in contact with them. It was clear that some of them were keen on taking more action around airports.

The big breakthrough, though, came in Birmingham. I was going up on the train to a conference on road building with an old friend from the anti-roads days, Jason Torrance. He was now working at Greenpeace. He said there were two young guys who would meet us off the train at New Street Station who might be interested in taking direct action against airports. That is when I first met Joss Garman and Richard George. Within weeks they were to become the co-founders of Plane Stupid. Lively, intelligent guys, driven by the threat of climate change, they both believed strongly that there should be a campaign of non-violent direct action against airports because aviation was the fastest-growing source of CO_2 emissions in the UK.

But Plane Stupid still wasn't a network. There were only four of us: Joss, Richard, myself and Graham Thompson, a good and experienced activist working at Greenpeace. That all changed at the first Climate Camp in 2006. The idea of a Climate Camp came from anti-roads activists of the 1990s who felt that the environmental direct action movement in the UK had become very fragmented. The Climate Camp was intended to bring activists together for a week to meet each other, share ideas about sustainable living and talk about the possibilities of taking direct action, particularly against industries which were emitting a lot of CO_2.

Climate Camp 2006

The first Climate Camp was held in a field outside the huge Drax Power Station a few miles from Selby in Yorkshire in the North of England. Plane Stupid was down to do a workshop. We knew this would be critical. Here were the nation's direct action activists. If we couldn't interest at least some of them in taking direct action against airport expansion, could we interest anybody? Joss and I could feel the tension as we sat on our straw bales in an empty tent waiting for somebody to come to our workshop. And then Leo Murray ambled in. Followed by some of his friends. And then some more activists. During the workshop Leo said airport expansion should and *could* be stopped through a campaign of direct action. Music to our ears! In the discussion which followed a lot of people showed a real interest in being part of such a campaign.

I had to get the train back to London that evening. I had a spring in my step as I walked to Selby station. I felt sure Plane Stupid was going places. I believed we now had our direct action network.

And so it proved. Within months Plane Stupid was hitting the national – and international – headlines with daring actions including the occupation of a taxiway at East Midlands Airport and the blockade of Easyjet's headquarters in Central London. But it was Heathrow that was to become the main focus of Plane Stupid's campaign.

A new generation of activists

This new generation of activists were similar to, but also different from, the protesters who had thrown themselves in front of bulldozers to stop motorways at Twyford Down and Newbury a decade earlier. There were two obvious differences. Plane Stupid focused exclusively on the threat of climate change. Secondly, Plane Stupid handled the media in a new way. Many of the direct action protesters of the 1990s, understandably suspicious of much of the mainstream media, gravitated towards the alternative media. Plane Stupid was equally sceptical of the motives a lot of the media but attempted to use it, even out-smart it, to get its point across and influence opinion.

Direct action becomes part of the Heathrow campaign

Plane Stupid became active in the Heathrow campaign. Activists, working alongside Seeds for Change, the organisation which assists community groups, helped train West London residents in direct action. These were local people, including a fair number of HACAN members, who had expressed an interest in taking direct action. The training led to a number of actions, including residents invading a major aviation conference in Central London where the Douglas Alexander, Secretary of State for Transport, was speaking. The purpose of these direct

West London residents join Plane Stupid in disrupting aviation conference in Central London. Photo: Russell

action events was two-fold. It was to put a warning shot across the bows of government that residents were willing to go further than ever before to stop expansion. But it also provided a an opportunity to identify and train up people who might be prepared to take part in a prolonged campaign of direct action should the expansion proposals not be dropped.

How the coalition operated: *Unity of Purpose; Diversity of Tactics*

Barbara Reid, a key figure who had both the ear of the Conservative Party and the respect of the young activists. Photo: Weedon

We are often asked questions how such a disparate group of organisations held together.

I think there were three reasons. One, we met face-to-face on a regular basis and so got to know and respect each other as individuals. Two, we were all utterly determined to win and somehow instinctively understood that winning was more important than any differences we might have. Three, each organisation contributed what it was good at and, critically, we understood that there were certain things that some of us could or would not do. Local authorities, for example, could not condone law-breaking. We understood and accepted that. Our slogan became: "Unity of Purpose; Diversity of Tactics." We usually met in the main offices of Hounslow Council, the most overflown borough in London. Our host was Councillor Barbara Reid, a leading member of the council which had just gone Conservative. Barbara was a pretty traditional Conservative. She found herself playing host to a variety of characters whom she wouldn't normally have come across. Quite rightly, she sought to establish some firm ground rules. Mutual trust emerged. We soon appreciated that by working together we had the greatest chance of winning. Barbara was to become an important figure in the campaign. She both had the ear of the Conservative Party and the respect of the young activists. She was one of those people who shaped the direction of the coalition and the campaign.

Developing our Arguments

Making the arguments against Heathrow expansion

In parallel with these direct action activities and the more conventional marches, demonstrations and public meetings, we put together the case against the expansion of Heathrow. The economic study was yet to come. But we had produced a short report which showed that many flights at Heathrow could be transferred to rail if a fast, affordable service was in place. Our study revealed that between a fifth and a quarter of all flights using Heathrow were to places where rail could be a viable alternative. The experience of many other European countries was that people would choose a good rail service which they could afford over flying for many of these short distances. If that happened at Heathrow, then many of the slots used by the short flights could be freed up to allow for any increase in long-haul flights from the developing economies of China and India which might be

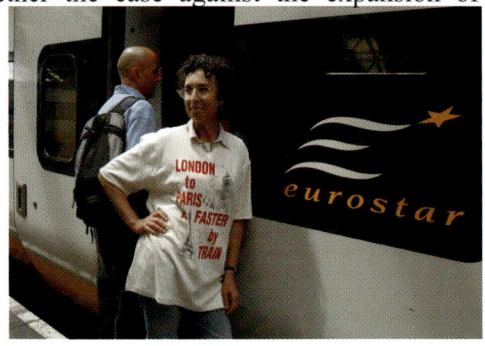

Our study into rail turned out to be influential in the months ahead. It showed that rail could be a viable alternative for up to 25% of flights using Heathrow. AiportWatch Co-ordinator Sarah Clayton modelling! Photo: Weedon

needed in the future, without having to expand the airport. This alternative was to prove important in influencing decision-makers and political parties over the coming years.

Speaking with the industry and Government?

We rarely spoke. What was there to say: they wanted a third runway, a sixth terminal and no runway alternation. We didn't. End of conversation.

I am often asked whether we spoke with the Government or the aviation industry. Our cross-party parliamentary group met with DfT civil servants and with the aviation ministers. This was most productive when Karen Buck was Aviation Minister. She was a thoughtful and independent-minded MP who resigned from her post, in part, it is thought, because of her dissatisfaction with government aviation policy. Some of the large national environmental organisations also had meetings with government ministers and civil servants, but mostly we did not. They showed no interest in speaking with us. That suited us fine. After all, what was there to say: they wanted a third runway, a sixth terminal and an end to runway alternation. We wanted none of those things. End of conversation.

Campaigning as part of AirportWatch

AirportWatch had developed a similar strategy at a national level. It sought to isolate the Department for Transport and the aviation industry. The strategy was beginning to work. A variety of think-tanks, scientists and academic institutions had produced reports which were highly critical of the Government's aviation policy. AirportWatch was also generating a lot of publicity, including ironic adverts, in national newspapers paid for by Enough's Enough.

Change within the Conservative Party

The Liberal Democrats and, not surprisingly, the Green Party had come out firmly against expansion at Heathrow. But, perhaps most interestingly of all, it was becoming clear that there could be some real movement in Conservative Party thinking. David Cameron, the new conservative leader had set up a Quality of Life Commission to look at a range of matters. The members of the Commission were not just drawn from the Conservative Party. They included a number of campaigners from AirportWatch as well as leading lights from the aviation industry. The transport section was chaired by the former transport minister Stephen Norris whom I had known in the 1990s and liked. He had done much to push sustainable transport policies within the Conservative Party. At the Quality of Life meetings it became clear that he saw the sort of airport expansion the Government was envisaging as deeply unsustainable, particularly in the light of its growing impact on climate change. He was opposed to a new runway at Heathrow. The final report of the Quality of Life Commission, though not taken on board as party policy, revealed that new thinking on aviation might well be emerging within the Conservative Party.

The tenacious Justine Greening, the Conservative MP for Putney, played an important role in the campaign from the early days.
Photo: Weedon

I just don't think the aviation industry believed it. Although invited to the Quality of Life Commission's meetings they seemed to put little serious effort into influencing them. I think they assumed that, whatever Stephen Norris might recommend, the traditional party of business would simply not oppose Heathrow expansion. They weren't alone in their thinking. I was taken out to lunch by a journalist from a left-leaning national newspaper. Towards the end of the meal he asked me what I thought would be the biggest single thing that would put pressure on the Government to drop Heathrow expansion. The Conservatives coming out against it, I said. He looked at me with something between bewilderment and pity. And I'm sure instantly regretted paying for the lunch! To him, too, it was inconceivable. But the journalist and the industry were blind to the signs that change was taking place within the Conservative Party.

It became clear that new thinking was emerging in the Conservative Party

We needed an economic report

The thinking emerging from the Conservatives made it all the more important that we got another key element of our strategy in place. For some time we had been looking for the money to commission a report which assessed the Government's claim that without a third runway the economy would suffer. It now became all the more urgent: it could help reassure the traditional party of business that the economic case for expansion was not a show-stopper. We got lucky. The Ashden Trust, one of the Sainsbury charitable trusts, offered us money. HACAN put in money. NoTRAG contributed £5,000. Greenpeace provided resources, including invaluable advice from Benet Northcote, a former City man and ex-Conservative Party candidate, working as their political adviser. Determined to commission an independent study, we deliberately avoided green or environmental consultants. We commissioned the Dutch economic consultancy, CE Delft, who had done work for the aviation industry, the European Commission as well as campaign organisations. The study wasn't questioning the important of Heathrow to the economy; simply whether expansion was essential for the UK economy as the Government and a lot of industry were claiming. We were hoping to publish the report just prior to consultation on Heathrow expansion, expected at the end of 2007.

Bart Boon, the main author of the CE Delft Report

BAA takes us to Court!

But first we were in for a very big shock. BAA was taking us to court! The Climate Camp had announced that it would be holding its 2007 week-long event in a field near Heathrow. As a tactic, it was magnificent….and the one which Plane Stupid had advocated. Well over a thousand of the nation's most committed direct action activists sleeping and plotting within sight of the Heathrow runways, just months before a major consultation into expansion was set to start. No wonder BAA and the Department for Transport were nervous.

BAA handed us the PR coup of a lifetime by trying to ban 6 million people from going to Heathrow or the 2007 Climate Camp

BAA's response was to take out a High Court injunction to stop us going to the Climate Camp or indeed anywhere near Heathrow Airport. I first heard about the injunction when I was on my way back from a meeting in Brussels. I was just passing between the two customs checks you need to go through before boarding Eurostar – the time you feel guilty even if you have done nothing wrong! – when my mobile rang. It was Paul Morozzo, an old friend from the anti-roads days and now an important figure in the climate camp movement. He told me I had been named in the injunction along with Joss Garman and Leo Murray of Plane Stupid and NoTRAG Chair Geraldine Nicholson. The injunction also named HACAN, NoTRAG, Plane Stupid and….. all members of AirportWatch supporting organisations.

Initial shock turns to elation

My first reaction was one of shock. This wasn't in the campaign plan! But then, as the train sped through the Belgian countryside, it dawned on me that BAA had gloriously, wonderfully overreached itself. By injuncting AirportWatch, BAA sought to ban over 6 million people! Amongst them, some of the most respectable in the land – members of organisations such as RSPB, CPRE and the National Trust, some of whom had the Queen as their patron. What's more, they sought to ban those 6million+ people not just from Heathrow Airport and the Climate Camp (in whichever field it might turn out to be), but from the Piccadilly Line, the M25, the M4 and platforms 6 and 7 at Paddington Station……indefinitely! I think the idea was to stop us getting to Heathrow. We will probably never know whether BAA or the Department for Transport, who it is rumoured put them up to this, actually knew what they were doing. I suspect they had little idea of who was part of the loose coalition known as AirportWatch. It was a great justification for operating as a loose association rather than a tightly controlled organisation.

I had to temper my excitement of the PR coup we had been handed in the knowledge that, if we lost, the resources of HACAN and other organisations might be under threat. I suspect that many of the large organisations were very unhappy about being dragged into the case but, to their credit, nobody broke ranks.

We were well represented in court by barristers from Matrix Chambers and solicitors from Harrison Grant and Friends of the Earth's legal team. As the trial went on we began to relax. It became clear that the judge, Mrs Justice Swift, a no-nonsense, eminently sensible woman from the English upper middle classes, was giving short shrift to BAA's over-the-top injunction. She was even a member of a number of the environmental organisations herself, she told us!

As we sat there, Joss Garman, Leo Murray and myself, we could only marvel at the media opportunity we had been handed. The world's press were listening as the court focussed on the names *HACAN*, *Plane Stupid* and *Heathrow*. This was press coverage to die for. Here was our issue in neon lights. Less than a year earlier we had been sitting on straw bales in a field outside Selby in Yorkshire. Thank you BAA!

Victory!

The judge dismissed the case against HACAN, NoTRAG, AirportWatch and Geraldine Nicholson. She granted a very limited injunction against Plane Stupid and the three of us. We were forbidden to go to or through Heathrow Airport around the time of the Climate Camp. We could attend the Climate Camp but not take direct action nor encourage others to do so. And costs were awarded against BAA.

BAA bolted out of court to tell the waiting media that they had got their injunction. Not quite true. They had

Leo Murray, John Stewart and Joss Garman celebrate outside the High Court. Photo: Weedon

got *an* injunction. But a million miles from the one they were looking for. What they had done was sky-rocketed our issue to the top of the political and media agenda.

It is fair to say that there were members of HACAN – and doubtless people in other organisations as well – who were deeply concerned about the court case. Some were concerned about our image; others about the potential threat to our relatively meagre resources. It was only right that I took on board these concerns. In the end of the day, I was there to represent the will of our members whatever my personal view about the unrivalled publicity the court case gave us.

The Climate Camp 2007 – in a field beside Heathrow!

Within weeks of the end of the court case, the Climate Camp began. Under cover of darkness, the campers had occupied a field just outside Sipson, the village that would have been demolished to make way for a third runway. It was very different from Selby a year earlier. The world's press was there. Pictures flew around the world. In the words of Linda McCutcheon, the Secretary of NoTRAG, this was the week "the campaign went global." The police presence was huge. There was tension in the air. This time I spoke to a packed workshop about Heathrow expansion.

The Climate Camp contains a wide range of people - workers, students, school-children, many young people but also some pensioners, all brought together because of a common concern about climate change. Some people take part in direct action throughout the year; many don't. But the Camp is a

valuable opportunity for people to meet and network. Local MP John McDonnell, who spent a night in a tent at the Camp, Liberal Democrat MPs Susan Kramer and Vincent Cable, all visited. The Camp had a positive effect on the residents of Sipson and the surrounding areas. Before the campers arrived, the local people didn't know what to expect. Many of them attended the Camp and liked what they saw. In fact, residents Jim Payne and his wife pitched a tent in the Camp which became a focal point for local people. After the Camp there was a new spirit in the villages. Residents now felt they could win. In their heart of hearts many of them had felt that ordinary folk like them couldn't take on the might of the aviation industry and government and win. After Climate Camp they knew they weren't alone. And we all knew the camp activists would return if the worst came to the worst and a third runway was imminent.

The impact of the Climate Camp on the campaign was momentous. Activists, politicians and local people talking about action and insurrection within sight of Heathrow and in the full glare of the world's media sent out the most powerful of messages.

The Political Support

One of the features of the campaign was that the Labour Party became totally isolated in its support for the third runway. The Conservatives and the Liberal Democrats were opposed. The Greens, as would be expected, were fierce opponents. But the smaller parties of both the left and the right, including those of the far left and the far right, also came out against it. Parties of the right, like UKIP and the British National Party (BNP) favoured closing down Heathrow and replacing it with a new off-shore airport. Their principle argument was that this would significantly reduce the number of people disturbed by noise. Parties of the left, like Respect, the Scottish Socialist Party, and the Trotskyite Socialist Workers Party were influenced by the impact climate change would have on working people both in the UK and abroad. These smaller parties of the left, along with some of the trade unions which were opposed to expansion like the RMT, (the rail workers union), and PCS, which represented many public sector workers, played an important role in developing the thinking on creating 'green' jobs. The obvious question is: why did the Labour Party dig its heels in and continue to support Heathrow expansion (even though many individual members of the Labour Party were against it)?

Political parties from the far right to the Marxist left all opposed expansion; why didn't Labour?

I suspect there may have been two reasons for this. Firstly, many in the Labour Party, very much including Gordon Brown, saw growth in old-fashioned terms. Brown had grown up with the assumption that new airports or new roads would bring jobs and prosperity. Their philosophy was to try and spread the fruits of that growth reasonably equitably but it was a given that this sort of growth was a good thing. Secondly, I think it had to do with misplaced notions of equity. The Labour Party clung to the view that 'working people' should have the same right to fly as better-off people. Thus, their defence of subsidised budget flights. This seemed to override everything else including the fact that some of the poorest communities in the land were plagued by aircraft noise and the certainty that climate change would hit the poorest people in the poor world first and most acutely.

The faith communities

We only had limited support from the faith communities. Individual churches, mosques and temples did support us. For example, a group of Christians, brought together by Harlington Baptist Church, showed their support at our events. And many individual people, motivated by their faith, joined us. The Archbishops of Canterbury and London sent messages of support. But the faith communities, as a whole were not prominent in the campaign. The official response from the Church of England was particularly disappointing, showing a marked reluctance to go against the business case for expansion. It may well have been lobbied effectively by Christians working within the aviation industry. Only belatedly did the London diocese publish a report critical of expansion. We believed that there were strong moral arguments to back up our case. We didn't, though, get this across to the faith communities as a whole.

November 2007: the official consultation starts

In November 2007, the Government started its official four month consultation. It was only into some aspects of expansion at Heathrow. But the details of their consultation document (for the record one of the most difficult to read ever produced and criticised by the Plain English Society) were not immediately relevant (they became much more so when we challenged the Government's decision in court; particularly over the absence of climate change) What mattered was how we used these four critical months. This was the time when the focus would be on Heathrow like never before. We dare not fail.

We had no intention of using the consultation in the traditional way. We intended to subvert *their* consultation to promote *our* agenda.

We had the coalition in place. But remember, we had no intention of using this consultation in the traditional way. We saw it as our big chance to put the issue of Heathrow expansion on the national agenda big-time. We intended to bombard the Government and the aviation industry with reports, demonstrations and public meetings; with research, direct action and colourful stunts. We intended to put them on the defensive. We intended to subvert their consultation to show our side of the story. During the consultation period the Department for Transport (DfT) held no public meetings and arranged for only a dozen or so one-day exhibitions to cover the whole of London and the South East. Of course we made a fuss about people not being properly consulted, as we did about the complexity of the consultation leaflet. But, in reality, it suited us fine. The more mistakes they made the better. We had no interest the Dft's 'fixed' consultation. For us, the purpose of the consultation was to promote our campaign.

The coalition comes into its own

The coalition came into its own. It organised over 40 public meetings across London and the Home Counties, attended by an estimated 20,000 people in total. The meetings were high-profile, with MEPs like the Green Party leader Caroline Lucas and the Liberal Democrat Sarah Ludford, joining MPs, council leaders and campaigners on the platforms. HACAN and NoTRAG held alternative exhibitions on the same day and in the same smart hotels as the DfT held theirs. They were none too pleased! Only one hotel refused us – we think under pressure from the DfT – so we settled for the smarter hotel down the road! Our exhibitions were to demonstrate that we weren't mere 'stakeholders' showing interest in the DfT's plans, but that we were equals with a valid and coherent vision of our own.

The coalition organised over 40 public meetings attended by an estimated 20,000 people in total

Green Party Leader Caroline Lucas, consistently helpful, spoke at a number of our meetings and rallies. Photo: Weedon

During the consultation period Greenpeace activists climbed on a plane at Heathrow Airport. Leaflets and literature were distributed widely, often by the local authorities. MPs kept up the pressure in the House of Commons. For a short period HACAN employed a lobbying consultancy, Cogitamus, which had good links with the heart of the Labour Party and the trade union movement. We had made big strides in influencing the opposition political parties. Many of the London Labour MPs were also onside. But we had made little headway with the heart of the Labour Party and the trade unions. Cogitamus's work was to bear fruit some months later when a significant number of Labour MPs they had spoken with rebelled against the Government's proposals.

HACAN and NoTRAG held alternative exhibitions on the same day and in the same smart hotels as the DfT to show we had a valid and coherent vision of our own.

Growing media coverage

We worked hard to get good media coverage of our activities. Key newspapers, from the liberal Guardian to Britain's biggest-selling quality Sunday newspaper, the more conservative Sunday Times and, perhaps critically for London, the London Evening Standard, came out against a third runway. I believe we only got the support of these serious newspapers because they understood that our campaign was not just based around colourful demonstrations and eye-catching actions, but that it was also rooted in sound arguments.

We publish our economics report

One thing was missing from our armoury at the start of the consultation. Our economics report was behind schedule. It wasn't until early 2008, two weeks before the end of the consultation, that it was ready for publication. It was essential for us that it was seen as a credible economic report; one that would win the respect of economists and business people. We launched it, therefore, not at Heathrow, or in a threatened village, or under the flight path, but in the City of London. We hired a room in the Stock Exchange where we served breakfast to an audience of business people and financial journalists. The launch was chaired by the former Conservative Transport Minister, Stephen Norris, now a successful businessman. The principal speaker was the main author of the report Bart Boon, from the Dutch consultancy CE Delft. The next day there was a long report about the report in Britain's premier business paper, the Financial Times.

> **The report dispelled the argument Heathrow expansion was essential for the economy. To stress the seriousness of the report we published it in the City of London.**

Although initially the aviation industry tried to rubbish the report, as we fully expected it would, we were confident we had a solid report. Over the coming year it turned out be a very important report indeed. It showed expansion of Heathrow was not essential for the health of the London or the UK economy. It found that, even if Heathrow did not expand, business was unlikely to relocate to other European cities with growing airports such as Frankfurt, Amsterdam and Paris because London had so much else to offer business. It also cast doubt on the industry's claims that unemployment would rise if Heathrow did not expand. It showed that, if people didn't spend their money on flying, they would spend it on something else, thus creating jobs in other sectors of the economy.

The report's findings proved invaluable at the public meetings during the consultation. At some of the meetings, the aviation industry was asked to provide a speaker. It was usually Clive Soley, a former MP and former Chairman of the Parliamentary Labour Party, who now headed up the pro-Heathrow expansion lobby group, Future Heathrow. Clive's mantra was that if Heathrow did not expand, business would go elsewhere in Europe and Heathrow would 'go the way of London's Docks' and be forced to close down. Using the findings of the CE Delft Report we were able to counter this with some authority.

Serious revelations put Government civil servants in a bad light

Some weeks before the consultation started, the Sunday Times revealed that civil servants at the Department for Transport had "colluded" with BAA when preparing for the consultation. They should have remained neutral. But minutes of meetings obtained by the Conservative MP for Putney, Justine Greening, showed how the civil servants had been in daily contact with BAA over ways in which the proposals for consultation could be presented in the best possible light. They discussed a 'rogue list' of people and organisations which would be obstacles in their drive for expansion. They included some local authorities. The revelations, which were to continue to seep out over the coming weeks and months as a result of further work by both Justine Greening and Greenpeace, were like gold-dust for us. Here was the close relationship between the Government and the aviation industry exposed for all to see. Here was the grubby secret world of the DfT civil servants spread across the pages of the national media. The Sunday Times even took the unusual step of naming a particular civil servant, David Gray, as being particularly involved in the process. This wasn't the image of a responsible government looking to build new infrastructure in the national interest. This was the story of dodgy deals with the aviation industry. At one point the civil servants had even asked BAA to go back and redo its figures so that the DfT could present expansion in a better light!

The Consultation ends in spectacular fashion

We had one big challenge left during the consultation period. We had booked the largest hall in Central Halls, Westminster, a well-known meeting venue in Central London, for an-end-of-consultation rally. We took an enormous risk. The hall held 2,500 people. We knew we had to fill it to make an impact. 1,000 people, normally regarded as a huge crowd for a meeting, would have looked like failure. As we had gone round our public meetings, we urged people to come and demonstrate their opposition to expansion in the famous venue, just across the road from Parliament and a stone's throw from the Department for Transport headquarters. That Monday evening, two and a half thousand people poured into the hall, with another five hundred in an overspill hall. As the band struck up, I looked across to NoTRAG's Geraldine Nicholson, who had done

3,000 people poured into Central London for the biggest indoor rally in our history. Photo: Weedon

so much to help organise it, and we both knew we had done it. The rally, chaired by our President Jenny Tonge, a champion of the cause for many long years, was addressed by local and national campaigners, environmental experts and a vast array of politicians including Nick Clegg, the leader of the Liberal Democrats. Although the rally was free, when we asked for donations, we raised a total of nearly £10,000, which paid for the cost of hiring the hall. An inspiring evening.

The link to Plane Stupid

Amongst the speakers was Leo Murray from Plane Stupid. Important his voice was heard. Even more important because he and I knew that two days later Plane Stupid was to mount its most spectacular action yet. Five young men and women, including Leo, got on to the roof of the Houses of Parliament. They draped a gigantic banner over the side saying, *BAA Headquarters*, to highlight the link between the Government and BAA. And they made paper aeroplanes out of the dodgy consultation document! That afternoon when addressing Parliament the Prime Minister, Gordon Brown, was forced to acknowledge their presence when he said decisions

On the last day of the consultation, two days after the rally, Plane Stupid protested on the roof of Parliament
Watch them up there:
www.youtube.com/watchv+EEH07GgMZI

should be taken on the floor of the House of Commons, not on the roof. It was the last day of the consultation. **Has ever a consultation ended so spectacularly?**

We hadn't played the consultation by the rules at all.

What the Government wanted was for us to spend long hours writing detailed responses to its proposals. We knew civil servants would hardly bother to read them. David Gray and the rest of the shamed civil servants had already made up their minds. They would just count how many people said 'yes' and how many said 'no'. So we urged people to respond simply. We advised them to 'just say no'. HACAN put in a brief response, no more. A consultation, which the Department for Transport had hoped would have focussed on their exhibitions and questionnaires, had been gloriously hijacked to give our campaign a buoyancy, vibrancy and visibility such as it never had before.

The Need to Maintain Momentum

We knew we had to maintain the momentum. It was essential to get across to the Department for Transport that for us its consultation was not an end in itself but simply a stepping stone to greater things. The coalition set about organising a major march and rally for early summer 2008 but, before that, we had two key events planned.

Staging an event with Stansted campaigners

Within weeks of the consultation, we put on a very different sort of event. In the Grosvenor Chapel in elegant Mayfair we staged, jointly with Stop Stansted Expansion (SSE), an evening of classical music. We had two key speakers: Terry Waite, the Anglican clergyman who had spent almost five years as a hostage in Lebanon, and Zac Goldsmith. This event was typical of the way we were working with campaign groups at other airports. Both SSE and ourselves were at a critical stage in our respective

Photo: Milligan

campaigns, yet we were determined to demonstrate our unity. The photo includes Zac Goldsmith (seated left), Terry Waite (seated right), Peter Sanders, SSE Chair (standing centre) and Carol Barbone, its Campaign Director.

Terminal 5 opens

The Heathrow consultation had ended on the 27th February 2008. Exactly a month later another big date loomed. Terminal Five was due to open. Long before I was involved in HACAN lots of our members had spent many long hours fighting Terminal Five. We knew that BAA, reeling from the revelations of its 'collusion' with the DfT and battered by its colossal misjudgement over the High Court injunction, would want to put on a big show. We needed to steal their thunder. Confrontation, though, would look bad. Plane Stupid-type direct action would not be inclusive enough if we were to involve an older generation who had fought Terminal Five. We needed something edgy but not confrontational; colourful but not just a photo-opportunity. And then it came to us: a Flash Mob!

We do a Flash Mob!

We had to advertise the Flash Mob in order to get people to Terminal 5, so the police and BAA were expecting something. As 11am approached familiar faces were milling around the new terminal and then.....on the dot of 11....more than 600 people revealed the red t-shirts they were wearing underneath their clothes emblazoned with the words *Stop Airport Expansion*. A sea of red filled the new terminal on BAA's big day. The worried authorities didn't know what we were going to do next. That was just the 'edge' we wanted. As it happened, after a bit of singing and dancing, we simply went home. As we had planned all along! The opening day of Terminal Five of course turned out to be a disaster for BAA and British Airways because the terminal wasn't working properly. Passengers were kept waiting. Flights were delayed. 23,000 bags went missing, many of them ending up in Rome. But for us, we had discovered a new, effective weapon in our armoury, the Flash Mob.

The Big May Rally

Our eyes now were on May 31st. The day of the big march we were planning near Heathrow, ending with a rally in Sipson, the village that would be destroyed if a third runway went ahead. Major events like this are only really possible with a coalition working together. Greenpeace took the lead in organising the event. Indeed, they put a huge amount of time, work and resources into it. On a hot Saturday in May, 3000 people marched and formed a big NO in a field in Sipson. We were joined by campaigners from Athens in Greece and Nantes in South West France. Leading politicians and environmentalists spoke at the rally hosted by John McDonnell, the local MP. Media coverage had been immense since the consultation. The press turned out in force. SKY News came live from the event - **click to see the video report** Heathrow Mass Protest   And yet we were disappointed with the numbers.

Photos: top left, Nutley; top right, Greenpeace; bottom left and right, Weedon

With an issue of this size and a campaign with this profile, there ought to have been thousands more people. One of the leading West London local papers, the Richmond and Twickenham Times, staunch supporters of the campaign, rang me after event to say they were going to run the front page headline, *Where Were You*? They were right to do so. We were thinking the same. We encountered little opposition to our campaign in West London or Berkshire. There was in fact a lot of support. The MPs in the areas and the local councils knew that their constituents would not forgive them if they failed to oppose expansion. And yet.......why were the numbers so low? Were people not bothered enough to come out? Or were they were not too comfortable marching? Perhaps they felt the campaign was going well enough that they wouldn't be missed, that other people, not them, went on marches? Or they felt that, however good the campaign was, it was doomed to failure? Perhaps it was a symptom of a broader issue: that these days many people feel that an afternoon at a protest march is an unwelcome intrusion into their busy lives? We may never know. It's probably something for academics to analyse. But my nagging doubts remained about how really important the issue was to the majority of people in West London. Buses had come from Manchester and Scotland. Why so relatively few from West London?

Many more than 3,000 should have turned up. Buses came from as far as Manchester and Scotland. The mystery remained: why so few from West London?

Summer 2008: the campaign progresses

Although the response in West London continued to be disappointing, more and more people were joining us from across the country. The high-profile nature of the campaign, together with a growing understanding of the huge impact a third runway would have, particularly on climate change, meant we were being contacted all the time by new individuals and groups keen to help. Much of the organisation of the Flash Mob, for example, had been done by young people who had joined us from the peace movement and the climate camp gatherings.

A new group, WeCAN, had emerged. It was based in one of London's smartest areas and was run by well-heeled women, concerned about what climate change would do to the world their children would grow up in. Amongst its organisers were Jennifer Nadel, former home affairs editor of ITN and the director and novelist Rebecca Frayn. Airport expansion was the catalyst for the group, but it's not the focus. But WeCAN became an active and valued part of the Heathrow Coalition. It also organised its own events, particularly involving children.

July 2008: An activist superglues himself to the Prime Minister!

As reported in the Times:
Dan Glass covered his hand with glue and placed it on the PM's sleeve at an awards ceremony at 10 Downing Street. He had smuggled the glue in in five pouches attached to his underwear and poured it over his hand during Mr Brown's speech. Mr Glass told the PM: "Do not worry, this is a non-violent protest. I have actually just superglued myself to the buttons of the Prime Minister. We cannot shake away climate change like you can just shake away my arm. We can beat climate change, but this is not going to happen by planning the world's largest international airport at Heathrow". Dan, a supporter of Plane Stupid, was given a round of applause by the other people in the room.

A radical conference is held

In July, some of the climate campers returned to the Sipson area for a day, almost a year since they had made international deadlines by pitching their tents within sight of Heathrow's runways. They joined forces with HACAN, NoTRAG and Greenpeace to organise a one day conference staged at the wonderfully supportive Harlington Baptist Church.

It brought together direct action activists, politicians, environmentalists and local residents.

The conference was part of a process of empowering a movement of people who might be prepared to engage in a sustained campaign of civil disobedience should the worst come to the worst. In some ways it may seem odd to talk like this just months after it became clear that the majority of West London residents were not prepared to march, far less take part in civil disobedience! But the sense of the people at the conference was that there were enough people out there – both residents and activists – for civil disobedience to be viable, if it was required.

Autumn 2008

The Conservatives come out against Heathrow Expansion

The Government was due to make its decision about Heathrow expansion towards the end of the year. Over the late summer I had worried the campaign was starting to lose a bit of momentum. But then came the phone call which changed everything. It was early Saturday evening. I had just come out of a pub in Bethnal Green in East London where I had watched the football on television. Newly-promoted Hull City had scored a famous victory over the mighty Arsenal. My mobile rang. It was Stephen Joseph, the Director of the Campaign for Better Transport (formerly Transport 2000). Excitedly he told me that he had just had a call from Theresa Villiers, the Shadow Secretary of State for Transport, to say that in her speech to the Conservative Party Conference the following week she would announce that, if the Conservatives won the next General Election, they would scrap all plans for Heathrow expansion and invest in high-speed rail instead. We had expected her to give us some encouraging signs on Heathrow but nothing like this. I wasn't to tell anybody. I didn't. Just! Sure enough, the speech was made. And it said the Conservatives would scrap all plans to expand Heathrow if elected and build a high-speed rail line instead. Gratifyingly, they used some of our statistics in justifying their view that a high-speed rail line would attract a fair number of people out of planes. As one senior national TV journalist said when he rang me to check the figures: "For your campaign, it doesn't get much better than this." My immediate reaction was that we had to be publicly very supportive in welcoming the announcement to counter the criticism the Conservatives would get from Labour, sections of industry, some trade unions and even from within their own Party. Over the next few weeks we ensured public support for the Conservative stance.

The Conservatives announced they would scrap all expansion plans if elected.

We seek business and trade union support

The pressing need was to get leading business figures to publicly support the Conservatives' stance. We knew the business community was divided over the issue but that there was a reluctance to break ranks. In fact it was to be another six months before leading business people came out publicly against the third runway. Six trade unions also came to oppose it. The business opposition, when it eventually did come, was very important to the campaign. It was almost unheard of for prominent leaders of business to oppose a major piece of national transport infrastructure like a third runway. The fact they chose to do so made their voice all that more persuasive.

The pressing need was to get business figures to publicly support the Conservatives' stance on Heathrow.

I was not the best person to lobby the business community. I was too much identified as a campaigner. Former business people like Chris Shaw from Enough Enough's, who had become a key part of the coalition, were much better suited to the role. And WWF, a more establishment NGO, published a ground-breaking report outlining the economic benefits of video-conferencing for businesses. In the case of the unions, the Campaign against Climate Change, one of the few environmental groups with strong links to the unions, did an important job of work. Once again the value of a broad-ranging coalition was demonstrated. The Conservatives' announcement also prompted the Government, which had previously rejected high-speed rail, to announce a study into it!

That autumn I was voted by the Independent on Sunday newspaper as Britain's most effective environmentalist. It covered my campaigning over the last 20 years or so. This included the campaigns against new roads as well as my contribution to the Heathrow Campaign. I was somewhat taken aback by the award. Recognition is always nice but my main thought was that it came at the perfect time to assist the campaign. It gave it some more publicity and probably put a touch more pressure on the authorities.

Winter 2008

That autumn another new group emerged, the Climate Suffragettes. It was really the brainchild of Tamsin Omond, who had first been active with Plane Stupid. It was a women-led group, though not exclusively made up of women, which focused on fighting climate change. It took its inspiration from the struggles of the Suffragettes battling for votes for women a century earlier. It organised the Climate Rush where, after a rally addressed by a number of women including the Leader of the  Green Party Caroline Lucas, the participants, many dressed as Suffragettes rushed Parliament to the bemusement of the Police. Another, different, and very useful front had opened up in the battle against Heathrow expansion.

Plane Stupid occupy Stansted

Meanwhile Plane Stupid was focusing on Stansted Airport which faced the prospect of a big increase in planes on the existing runway as well as the construction of a second one. Under cover of darkness on a freezing cold December night, over 100 activists from Plane Stupid broke through the fence to occupy the taxiway at Stansted Airport. It was the biggest occupation of an airport ever seen in this country. Flights were cancelled. Passengers were angry. Some of the media were furious. This was the first time that Plane Stupid had disrupted passengers. They thought carefully before doing so, but decided that the problems of inconveniencing passengers were outweighed by the threat of climate change and by the message that had to be sent to the Government and the aviation industry: new runways will be met by resistance. The action was very different to the style of campaigning being led by Carol Barbone, the dynamic Director of Stop Stansted Expansion (SSE), who had turned a sleepy campaign into one of the most respected in the land, building up a good team around her, including people like the former businessman Brian Ross, who was so important to both the Stansted campaign and to AirportWatch in developing a coherent economic case against expansion. SSE had always avoided the direct action route - hence the stir which was created when Plane Stupid decided to take a different approach.

The biggest occupation of an airport yet seen in the UK

Labour MPs rebel as D-Day draws near

Susan Kramer MP was an important and committed figure in the campaign. She headed up the Lib Dem opposition. Photo: Weedon

The Government's decision on Heathrow was expected before the end of the year. But they were in difficulties. There were signs of a revolt within the Labour Party. The work that our consultancy Cogitamus had done was bearing fruit. A number of the MPs whom they had spoken to were at the forefront of the revolt. Over 100 Labour MPs signed Early Day Motions opposing expansion. Alan and Ann Keen, mainstream Labour MPs who were part of our cross-party group, spoke to others within their Party. In parliamentary debates Labour MPs were voting against the Government. The Government was experiencing further trouble in these debates as both Theresa Villiers for the Conservatives and the Liberal Democrat Transport Spokesman Norman Baker consistently made a sound environmental and economic case against expansion. More than once they cited our CE Delft report on economics. On each day that there was a debate or motion on Heathrow, we mustered a visible presence outside Parliament, sometimes at very short notice. We could usually rustle up about 60 people, enough for a good story and a picture for the media. The Government announced that the decision would not be made until the New Year. The Cabinet was split.

The decision was postponed until January as the Cabinet was split

January 2009 – Decision is Made

We knew we had to hit the ground running in January. The intense pressure on the Government had to be maintained. The Climate Rush and WeCAN planned a dinner on the first day MPs came back…..on the concourse of Terminal 1 at Heathrow! And we intended to stage another Flash Mob on the first Saturday after the decision was announced.

Maintaining the pressure

The dinner party was enormous fun. People came in their hundreds, many in smart early 20th Century costumes. Women from the Suffragettes; mothers from WeCAN; children from the threatened communities; West London residents; environmental campaigners; Plane Stupid activists. At least two of our cross-party group of MPs - John McDonnell and Susan Kramer – were there. With table clothes spread across the concourse of Terminal I, under the watchful eye of masses of Police, people ate their picnics, consumed their drinks, sang, danced and partied. As I watched the scene unfold, I got the overwhelming sense that, if need be, many of these people would be singing and dancing on the runways of the airport if ever required.
You can join the dinner: http://wwwyoutube.com/watch?v=G6h9vChzxhM&geature=related

The next day, to keep up the pressure, Greenpeace launched **Airplot** - a brilliant idea where a number of celebrities bought a piece of land from a local businessman in the threatened village of Sipson. They then gave away bits of that land to anybody who wanted them.

Government announces its decision

A few days later, the Government announced its decision. It dropped plans to do away with runway alternation - the practice where planes landing over West London switch runways at 3pm in order to give residents a half day's break from the noise. This was a major triumph: again it is thought cross-party group members, Alan and Ann Keen, used their influence with government to help bring this about. But BAA was given the green light to draw up plans for a third runway. However, in order to get the decision through a divided Cabinet, the Transport Secretary Geoff Hoon announced that, if it became clear by 2020 the third runway was likely to exceed the limits for noise, air pollution or emissions the Government had laid down, the number of planes using the new runway would be capped. A messy, and probably unworkable, compromise. Two West London Labour MPs, Andy Slaughter and Virendra Sharma, resigned from their Government jobs in protest at the decision. Both became part of our cross-party group. The announcement was front page news of course. We had forced Heathrow to the top of the political agenda. The coalition staged a press conference, televised live, within hours of the announcement in the elegant offices of the National Trust.

> **Amongst uproar and resignations it gave the green light for the 3rd runway**

John McDonnell takes direct action in the House of Commons

In the House of Commons there was uproar. John McDonnell got so angry at Geoff Hoon's refusal to give him straight answers that he left his seat, strode down the isle of the House of Commons and seized the Mace. A totally illegal act! Direct action on the floor of Parliament! He was suspended for a week. He returned to his constituency to a standing ovation.   Watch what happened: John McDonnell suspended from house of commons 15th January 2009

Over 70,000 consultation responses: only 11% in favour

The Government admitted it had received over 70,000 responses to the consultation, thought to be the greatest ever number to regional consultation. Only 11% favoured expansion. The discredited civil servant David Gray sneered that he had expected more responses! By this stage the man had become a major liability for the DfT and a gift to our campaign. It is no surprise that within months the Department moved him to "other duties".

Our response

Within days of the decision hundreds of people descended on Heathrow for another Flash Mob in Terminal 5. Once more we revealed our red t-shirts. This time we belted a cardboard cut-out of Geoff Hoon with coloured sponge balls! Geoff Hoon, one of the most unpopular Government ministers, was the perfect villain for us. His predecessor, Ruth Kelly, was a highly principled and personally decent woman. We just disagreed with her policies. We found Geoff Hoon simply disagreeable! When fighting a campaign like this, it is so much easier to take on a real villain!

The Flash Mob concept was working. Edgy but inclusive. And enormous fun. Politicians began to take part. Vincent Cable MP, the Liberal Democrats respected economics spokesperson, came to some. As did Jenny Jones, a leading Green Party member of the London Assembly; and Murad Quereshi, the Labour Chair of its Environment Committee. John McDonnell and the Liberal Democrat MP Susan Kramer were at most of them. **Above, Armelle Thomas and Eilish Stone, two of the women from Harmondsworth, who had become stalwarts of the campaign.**

Post-decision: the need to keep the momentum going

The challenge after any big decision, particularly when the build-up to it is as high-profile as this one was, is to keep the momentum going. But a strange thing happened. As the months past, we began to realise that Geoff Hoon's decision was pretty irrelevant. By March 2009, more than a year before the General Election, I felt sure we had won the campaign. Gordon Brown's Labour Party was looking certain to lose the Election. It had become plain that the Conservatives were serious about their plans to scrap a third runway. They were making it a major plank of party policy. Theresa Villiers, their transport spokeswoman, had said it would feature as a key part of their Election Manifesto. It was also becoming clear that they would drop plans for new runways at Stansted and Gatwick. They favoured some expansion at regional airports. The Liberal Democrats had a very similar policy. BAA had made it clear they wouldn't have the detailed plans for a third runway ready before the Election. The media largely lost interest in the third runway. It was no longer a story. They, like most people, believed it just wouldn't happen. We were in an odd situation, one I had never been in before in 30 years of campaigning. We had won great battles but our victory wouldn't be confirmed for at least a year. But we needed a plan of action for the year.

We develop a three part strategy

We developed a three part strategy. First, we drew up plans to ensure that Heathrow remained in the public and media eye. As part of this we decided to mount a legal challenge to the Government's decision to give the third runway the go-ahead. Second, we worked on the rail alternatives to Heathrow Expansion. And third, we prepared for the unlikely eventuality of Labour winning the election.

Strategy Part 1: Keep Heathrow in the public eye

A lot of the activities centred round Airplot
http://www.youtube.com/watcv+2JDe3lRuj10

Various members of the coalition organised a series of reasonably co-ordinated activities to keep Heathrow in the public eye. A lot of those activities revolved around Airplot. Over 90,000 people eventually "bought" a piece of land; in effect a blade of grass each! During the year a stream of celebrities came to visit Airplot, including the Poet Laureate and the veteran comedy star Richard Briers. The Conservative leader David Cameron sponsored at tree on it. The Liberal Democrat leader went one better and came and planted his tree! All great photo-opportunities. All ways of keeping Heathrow in the media. But it also meant that, if the new Government, had gone ahead with the runway, Nick Clegg would have had to serve a compulsory purchase order on himself!

A Euro Flash Mob

We did another Flash Mob. Each Flash Mob had to be a little different. This time we did a European Flash Mob. We contacted campaign groups at other airports in Europe and a number of us did a Flash Mob at our airports on the same day. On a day of real significance for Europe - the morning of the Eurovision Song Contest! Each campaign group sang their country's entry. We looked and sounded superbly tacky! It was great fun. But we decided it was to be our last Heathrow Flash Mob. It had lost its edge. BAA and the Police now knew what we did and

Photo: Russell

were too comfortable with it. It was in danger of just becoming another photo-opportunity. We always had known that our Flash Mobs would have a limited, if colourful, life. It was time to stop.

Other events took place. The Campaign against Climate Change staged a sizeable demonstration outside Downing Street. Amongst the speakers was Linda McCutcheon from NoTRAG. She who never saw herself speaking in public was addressing the crowds outside Downing Street! WeCAN and the Climate Rush put on events. But probably the most eye-caching stunt was when Leila Deen from Plane Stupid threw green custard over the senior Cabinet Minister Peter

Leila Deen, from Plane Stupid, throws green custard over third runway-supporting Cabinet Minister Peter Mandleson

Mandelson, telling him that, as long as he supported a third runway, his policies were 'greenwash'. Mandelson was the perfect target: a slimy character, a known supporter of the third runway, and one of the most famous faces in British politics. The press lapped it up. It became one of the pictures of 2009. When Plane Stupid does something like this, it makes a lot of people smile. It also makes a lot of people very annoyed. Many of the angry comments are along the lines of "this won't change anything". Of course it won't. Not by itself. But, as part of the wider campaign, which the Plane Stupid actions always are, it is different story.

Mount a legal challenge

The coalition mounted a legal challenge against the Government's decision. We argued that the way it was arrived at was unlawful. Campaigners usually lose legal challenges and they can be very expensive so they need to be thought about very carefully. On this occasion we felt that a challenge would keep the issue in the public eye and increase pressure on the Department for Transport. With generous help from key local authorities, it was affordable. It turned out to be the right decision – as we were to discover almost a year later.

Strategy Part 2: The Rail Alternative

Barbara Reid outside the Scottish Parliament after giving evidence on behalf of 2M on high-speed rail

The second area we concentrated on was rail. The Government had set up a committee to come up with a high-speed rail scheme. But it simply looked like political opportunism. It had seen the Tories and the Liberal Democrats make the running on rail. Gordon Brown needed a study to wave around before the General Election. Labour didn't regard high-speed rail as an alternative to a 3rd runway at Heathrow. The Government scoffed at the idea it would take people off planes. It put Sir David Rowlands in charge of the study. Remember him! He had been the Permanent Secretary at the Department for Transport, its chief civil servant, during the time the Government was developing and promoting its expansionist aviation policies. He now chairs the Board of Gatwick Airport. He was to be assisted by Alison Munro, another DfT civil servant, who became notorious for her stone-walling answers many years earlier at the Terminal 5 Inquiry. I felt we should have as little to do with the study as possible. The local authorities, though, had little choice but to speak with Rowland's team. Some of the NGOs chose to do so. The coalition did its own work on high-speed rail. 2M published a study. We liaised with the Liberal Democrats and the Conservatives – they both saw rail as an alternative to Heathrow expansion.

Strategy Part 3: Be ready for an unexpected Labour Election win

We had to start preparing the ground should Labour unexpectedly win the General Election, still a year away. There was always the possibility that, with the Party divided on the issue, Labour would drop a third runway post-Election. But, with Gordon Brown so keen on it, we had to assume they would try to push ahead. Traditionally, we would have started preparing for a Public Inquiry. We didn't do that. The lessons of history told us that, if we reached public inquiry stage, we had probably lost. We went down a different route. Some of us quietly began to prepare for a campaign of civil disobedience. It had to be done largely behind the scenes. A wise Tory MP had said to me that it would not help the Conservatives deal with dissenters within their own Party if there were pictures of people invading Heathrow splashed across the television screens prior to a General Election.

There were plans in preparation for mass civil disobedience

Activists pledge to help residents defend their homes

For video of event click **Adopt a Resident**   Photo: Pushinsky

Our work revolved around direct action activists getting to know local residents, particularly in the threatened villages in the NoTRAG area. A number of Plane Stupid activists moved into houses in the area and set up direct action training sessions. But they also became part of the community, staging film shows, taking part in local carnivals and regenerating derelict sites (such as the imaginative *Grow Heathrow* site, cultivated by Transition Heathrow, **photo below**). Important friendships were formed. One of the early events where activists and residents got to know each other took place in St Mary's Church Hall, the 11th century Parish Church in Harmondsworth, where individual residents were 'adopted' by activists. Later in the autumn a Ceilidh – similar to a barn dance – was organised by activists who came down from Scotland. Heathrow residents were being 'adopted' by activists from across the UK. The activists were welcomed into a community which had become worn down by nearly ten years of struggle. Some residents were selling their homes to BAA. There were real fears that the fabric of the community might fall apart. Once again, as after the Climate Camp, activists helped reassure residents they were not on their own. More widely, Heathrow had become such an iconic battle in the fight against climate  change that thousands of activists from across the country were ready to descend on the airport if a third runway was not dropped.

AirportWatch in 2009

By 2009 things had changed for AirportWatch as well. It had played a key role in both pushing aviation matters up the political agenda and highlighting the economic and environmental impacts of expansion. Its reward was that both the Conservatives and Liberal Democrats had pledged to rule out new runways at Heathrow, Stansted and Gatwick.

In March 2009 AirportWatch held a supporters' conference to assess the new situation and map out a fresh strategy. The battle had moved away from the big three airports in the South East to the Scottish and regional airports, including the smaller airports in the South East, such as London City Airport. I wrote a booklet outlining why I believed the expansion of regional airports didn't work at an environmental or economic level. The argument was based on three things. One, the increased number of flights would bring noise problems, in some places for the first time. Two, the total amount of CO_2 emissions produced by all regional airport flights was very significant. Three, regional expansion was not helping the regional economies because the planes were taking more people and money out of the regions than they were bringing in. This was largely due to the tourist deficit – British people flying abroad were spending more money there than visitors spent in this country. This regional aviation deficit ran into billions each year. Only 25% of trips at regional airports were for business purposes.

> The battle had moved from the big three airports in the South East to the Scottish and regional ones

AirportWatch argued that, instead of expanding airports, investment should be directed towards new 'green' jobs. The interesting thing was that the left in politics, in some cases the far left, was calling for something very similar to many on the right. *One Million Climate Jobs Now!*, produced by the Campaign against Climate Change for three leading trade unions and Zac Goldsmith's book, *The Constant Economy: How to create a stable society* sought similar outcomes. The means of getting there, of course, were different – Zac favoured fiscal and market-led solutions; the trade unions were looking much more towards direct government investment. For all his slogans, Gordon Brown hadn't even reached the foothills of this debate.

AirportWatch's decision to take part in this debate around green jobs raises the interesting question about how far single-issue campaigns should get involved in wider issues. My own view is that campaigners have to think very carefully before going beyond their own remit. The thing that binds very different people in a campaign together is their specific campaigning issue: be it opposition to airports; or roads; or whatever. To go beyond that, risks breaking that bond. However, when the wider issue adds to the strength and range of your campaign, there is a clear benefit in getting involved. As a campaign organisation, AirportWatch has no view on such matters as fox-hunting, gay rights, the death penalty or abortion. Equally, it has no party political affiliation. But it is interested in investment in green jobs because those are sources of alternative employment if growth in aviation is to be scaled back or halted. To get involved makes us a more coherent campaign with a more rounded message.

> AirportWatch supported investment in green jobs instead of airport expansion

By 2009, then, the aviation debate had moved on. The ruling in the Heathrow Court case would move it on still further and have more implications for the direction of AirportWatch's work. But that was still a year away.

Summer/Autumn 2009: The industry attempts to fight-back

In the second half of 2009 the aviation industry made what looked like one last effort to influence the Conservative Party. The British Chamber of Commerce published a study it had commissioned from the transport consultancy, Colin Buchanan. The study claimed that a third runway would bring benefits to the UK economy at least six-fold greater than even the Department for Transport dared claim! But careful scrutiny of the study showed up major flaws. The industry tried to use the study as the basis of a national tour of the country to persuade regional business leaders of the benefits of a third runway, but it was too late. The aviation industry had failed to convince the Conservatives. It had badly misjudged the Conservative Party. It had assumed it would be onside. So it had gone all out to influence New Labour. The aviation industry had brought in many of its key lobbyists from the heart of the Labour Party: Dan Hodges, the Director of Freedom to Fly, the first pro-expansion pressure group, was the son of the former Labour Aviation Minister, Glenda Jackson. Prior to 1997 he had been part of the Millbank team which worked to get New Labour elected; Stephen Hardwick, the Head of Public Affairs for many years at BAA, was another Millbank stalwart; Jo Irwin, Hardwick's successor at BAA, was formerly John Prescott's right-hand man; Clive Soley, Director of Future Heathrow, was a past Chairman of the Parliamentary Party; Michelle di Leo, the head of Flying Matters, the latest pro-expansion pressure group, was the wife of Dan Hodges. All these people had been brought in to lobby and influence a Labour Government. They were well-suited to do that. But could these people, so associated with the Labour Party, ever be effective lobbyists of the Tory Party? The problem I think went even deeper. These lobbyists thought like the Labour Government. They had the same mind-set as Ruth Kelly, Geoff Hoon and Gordon Brown. I'm not sure they could accept in their own minds there was a realistic and equitable alternative to Labour's aviation policy. They almost functioned as a wing of government. Somebody like Willie Walsh, the boss of British Airway, was able to put the case for expansion with a clarity and conviction that was absent from most of the industry lobbyists and a million miles from the stonewalling tactics of the Department for Transport civil servants.

> The aviation industry lobbyists, many of them plucked from the heart of the Labour Party, were ill-suited to lobby the Conservatives

Josh from Plane Stupid and NoTRAG's Tracy storm the stage of the Architects Awards to warn firms who may bid for 3rd runway work that they would face direct action

In the Summer of 2009, BAA, too, spluttered to life with one last effort. It said it would buy up the homes of people in Sipson who wanted to move out. A few people had been agitating to go for some time, but this move by BAA just had the effect of destabilising the community. BAA also appointed the self-styled 'green' architects, Grimshaws, to design the new runway. Plane Stupid, accompanied by Tracy, the barmaid from the King William 1V pub in Sipson, stormed the stage of the Architects Annual Awards Ceremony, in protest. A few weeks earlier Plane Stupid, along with NoTRAG's Christine Taylor, had occupied Virgin's table at another prestigious awards ceremony in protest against Virgin's support for a third runway. The stunts were entertaining but they had a serious purpose: to warn companies which supported or hoped to get work from the building of a third runway that they would be prime targets in any campaign of civil disobedience. But in truth the campaign was winding down. By the start of 2010 we were counting the days to a General Election.

2010 Brings a Surprise

We win our court case! Above, MPs Susan Kramer, John McDonnell, Justine Greening and Councillor Barbara Reid, flanked by key council leaders and campaigners, emerge victorious from the High Court. The judge had found that the Government's decision in 2009 to give BAA the green light for the third runway was flawed. He ruled that it did not take into account the most recent evidence on climate change and economics because it was based on the 2003 Air Transport White Paper. He also ruled that insufficient work had been done on how the extra passengers using a third runway would get to and from the airport. We weren't out of the woods yet. But this was a severe setback for the Government. It had to go back to square one to make the case for the third runway. More than that, the ruling gave hope to all groups facing expansion across the country as the vast majority of the expansion proposals were based on the Air Transport White Paper which the judge said was outdated.

It remains very rare for campaigners to win in the courts. Never put all you faith in the courts! If you go to law, see it as just one element in the overall campaign. But, occasionally, there is a victory. In our case it was down to a superb team of lawyers (our solicitors, Kate Harrison and her colleagues from Harrison Grant; our barristers, Nigel Pleming, Natalie Lieven and colleagues from Landmark Chambers) well-briefed by the local authority officers and the campaigners; a woeful case being put forward by the discredited Department for Transport; and an intelligent judge bold enough to find against the Government. A rare mix!

The General Election result seals it

Less than two months later Labour had lost the General Election. The Conservatives, though, were denied an outright win. They had to form a coalition with the Liberal Democrats. The day after the new Government was formed, it announced a 3rd runway would be scrapped. It also said it would block new runways at Stansted and Gatwick. Never in UK history had the aviation industry suffered such a rebuff. Our campaign had ensured that Heathrow was a key issue for the new Government. Indeed, one of its first decisions was to announce its proposal to scrap it. Interestingly, it appears the Labour Party in its vain attempt to hold on to power by doing a deal with the Liberal Democrats was willing to drop its plans for a third runway in order to tempt the Liberal Democrats into coalition.

ANALYSIS

Tom Edwards, BBC London's Transport Correspondent

That unlikely alliance of campaigners - the councils, the residents and environmentalists - have won. It was always common ground between the Conservatives and the Liberal Democrats to oppose the third runway. A campaigner I've met many times over the years said she could not stop crying when she heard the news this afternoon. There will be parties tonight......

The day after the night before

It was the day after the Government made its announcement. By coincidence, the day Greenpeace had planned to hand in to the Prime Minister at 10 Downing St the names of the 90,000 people who had bought part of the Airplot field in Sipson as a protest against a third runway. Instead it turned into a celebration……

Anna Jones and Ben Stewart of Greenpeace, and NoTRAG's Linda McCutcheon outside 10 Downing St.

Facing the nation's media

And skipping with sheer joy down Britain's most famous street. We've done it!

Photos: Greenpeace

Reflections on the Campaign..................

I think there were eight key elements which contributed to our success:

1. We started early. Bodies like BAA and international industries like aviation plan well in advance. The Civil Service, too, can have long-term plans. The trick of government and industry is often to let local people know of their plans at the last minute making long-term planning difficult. But the ideal is to start early. Plan strategically. Plan for the long-term.

2. We rejected Nimbyism (Not in My Backyard). It would have been impossible to have made the wider economic and climate change arguments coherently, or make a case for a rail alternative and a transition to green jobs, it we were arguing that that expansion should take place elsewhere. Our ability to develop these wider arguments enabled our campaign to challenge the industry more effectively and to be taken more seriously by politicians.

3. We worked in a broad coalition. The coalition obviously increased our numbers but it also meant we were able to campaign effectively on a greater range of issues - noise, climate change, community destruction, economics, rail alternatives, and biodiversity – and using a wider range of tactics, from Parliamentary lobbying to direct action.

4. We didn't avoid economics. Too often campaigners avoid tackling economics because it seems too daunting or because it doesn't interest them. This is a mistake because the reason put forward for many of the developments they are opposing is economic. The fact that we were able to shed real doubt on the strength of the economic argument being put forward for Heathrow expansion was a critical factor in stopping it.

5. We set the agenda. We did not wait simply to respond to official consultations and give evidence at public inquiries. We set the pace through creative, pro-active campaigning. We tried to put the other side on the defensive through highlighting their flaws, publishing our own reports and co-ordinating a series of high profile events and actions.

6. We identified our allies. We sought people and organisations which might support us. We cultivated their support. This way we established good working relationships with the opposition parties, those trade unions who were interested in 'green' jobs, and many others.

7. We didn't waste time on our enemies. This is not to say that campaigners should never talk to those they are battling against but only talk to them if it is in your interest to do so. Those in authority often love to consult and talk to us in order to bog us down in details and waste out time. Don't fall for it! Sometimes, though, in a broad coalition, it can be useful for some members of it - like elected representatives for example – to talk to the other side while the rest of the coalition gets on with the pro-active campaigning.

8. We spent many hours on the campaign. Not everybody is in the position to campaign full-time but, without a huge number of hours put in by many people, this campaign could not have been effective. Campaigning is disruptive of daily life. But it is a necessary part of any successful campaign. At its peak some of us were working over 100 hours a week.

> **Finally, if there is one thing I'm asked about more than any other is the direct action**. It's illegal – and that worries people. It's eye-catching – and that can lead to the perception that direct action is all a campaign is about. It wasn't direct action alone that won this campaign. The mustering of solid arguments, the persistence of local communities, the diligence of local authority officers, the intelligent use of the political process all played critical roles. But it would have been a very different campaign without the direct action. The direct action campaigners dramatised the campaign. They also provided much of the energy and creativity behind many of the campaign's other activities, such as the Flash Mobs, and their presence made very real the threat of civil disobedience if the expansion plans were not dropped. I'm not at all certain we would have been drinking champagne if the direct action activists had been missing from the campaign.

"Impossible is just an opinion"

I'm not sure who first said that. But we do feel we have achieved the near-impossible. We hope our story has shown that it is not impossible to stop a new runway being built at an airport. We trust it will give hope and inspiration to campaigners around the world who are fighting new runways. Or indeed major unwanted developments of any sort.

We have stopped the runway. But what we haven't done is halt the gradual increase in flight numbers on the existing runways. Most airport campaigners are not faced with a new runway. Most are fighting a steady increase in the number of planes using the airport or extensions to the airports, perhaps an extended runway or an expanded terminal. These less dramatic proposals are proving harder to defeat. We had very clear plans for expansion to mobilise around. Without such plans, it is proving harder to get campaigns off the ground. That maybe is the next challenge facing all of us.

Where now for HACAN……

HACAN has been part of a famous victory. But we have work yet to do. The planes are still roaring over our heads. During the years of the campaign the noise has become immeasurably worse for many people. Planes are lining up to join their final approach path much further out than before. Aircraft noise is now a real problem for more people much further from the airport. **Just listen to this video: Under The Flight Path Crossroad** The Labour Government ignored all pleas to do anything about it. For these people the victory in the third runway campaign will ring very hollow indeed if nothing is done about the sky of sound over their heads. For some people further east, the problem has been compounded by changes in flights paths from London City Airport. HACAN has formed an alliance with the local campaign group at City Airport, Fight the Flights. And then there are night flights. Something else the Labour Government refused to do anything about. Indeed, it went all the way to the European Court of Human Rights to defend them. More campaigning to do. But it will be taking place in a new political climate, with a more sympathetic government in power.

And the perhaps the final challenge, the toughest test of any campaign: has it brought about lasting change? Only time will tell but the omens are looking good. Three runways have been dropped – at Heathrow, Stansted and Gatwick. The campaigners at the three airports fought together, and won together. More than that, a new approach to aviation policy is emerging, one that is more critical of the aviation industry, a less expansionist approach. If that new approach takes off, it could see the start of the old attitudes grounded for good.

Notes and References

(1). The quote is from a wonderful book, *Heathrow, 2000 Years of History*, by local historian Philip Sherwood.

(2). At the Election Ann Keen lost her seat to the Conservative Mary Macleod and Zac Goldsmith won Richmond Park for the Conservatives.

The front cover photo is from Greenpeace

About the author

John Stewart was a central figure in the successful campaign to stop a third runway at Heathrow Airport. He chaired the local campaign group and played a key role in bringing together the most wide-ranging coalition of organisations and individuals ever assembled in the UK to oppose a new runway. He also chaired AirportWatch, the national umbrella body of organisations opposed to airport expansion across the country.

He has been campaigning on transport and environment issues for nearly thirty years. He chaired ALARM, the coalition of over 200 community groups, which defeated Government plans in the 1980s for a multi-billion progamme of road building schemes in London. In the 1990s he was prominent in the national 'anti-roads' movement which forced the Government to scrap hundreds of road schemes.

He is a former Chair of Transport 2000 and of the road safety charity, RoadPeace. He currently chairs the UK Noise Association and is a Vice Chair of UECNA, the European body which represents airport campaign groups.

In 2008 he was voted the UK's most effective environmentalist by the newspaper, the Independent on Sunday.

ISBN: 978 0 85124 7892

Printed by the Russell Press Ltd., Nottingham

Published by HACAN, PO Box 339, Twickenham, TW1 2XF; tel 020 8876 0455; email info@hacan.org.uk; www.hacan.org.uk   Revised version: December 2010